a year of AFGHANS
1996

LEISURE ARTS, INC.
and
OXMOOR HOUSE, INC.

With A Year of Afghans *at your fingertips, you'll have 52 beautiful wraps to fill your calendar with crochet! Inside this premier volume in our annual series, you'll find a timeless treasury of warmth for marking special days — or any day.*

Stroll through the seasons, month by month, and discover all the plushness, all the texture, all the color that handmade afghans have to offer. Chase away winter's chill with an Aran classic or a log cabin design. Crocheted tulips, daffodils, orchids, and daisies make breezy comforts for spring days. You can create something blue for a June bride, or while away the summer with ocean-side shells. Our autumn styles capture rich harvest hues and can spark that home-team spirit. And a blanket of snowflakes or an evergreen inspiration will provide a wonderful year-end wrap-up.

Of course, we didn't forget the holidays! Whether made to keep or to share, these designs are lovely for charming a valentine, "egging on" the Easter bunny, and saluting patriotic days. A bounty of harvesttime texture befits a Thanksgiving throw, and a snowy pal will deck the halls with Yuletide tradition.

Our step-by-step stitch guides and handy diagrams mean that both beginning and advanced crocheters can enjoy a variety of easy-to-follow patterns. So grab your hook and get ready to embark on a new crocheted creation each and every week!

table of contents

FROSTY FLOWERS

Plush popcorn stitches create the snowy white flowers on this cozy wrap! The frosty look is accentuated with worsted weight yarn in two icy blue shades.

Finished Size: 51" x 68"

MATERIALS

Worsted Weight Yarn:
   White - 58 ounces,
      (1,650 grams, 3,265 yards)
   Blue - 19 ounces,
      (540 grams, 1,070 yards)
   Lt Blue - 15 ounces,
      (430 grams, 845 yards)
Crochet hook, size H (5.00 mm) **or**
   size needed for gauge
Yarn needle

GAUGE: Each Square = 5¹/₂"

SQUARE (Make 108)

Note #1: To work **beginning Popcorn**, ch 3, 3 dc in st or sp indicated, drop loop from hook, insert hook in top of beginning ch-3, hook dropped loop and draw through.

Note #2: To work **Popcorn**, 4 dc in st or sp indicated, drop loop from hook, insert hook in first dc of 4-dc group, hook dropped loop and draw through *(Fig. 10a, page 137)*.

With White, ch 8; join with slip st to form a ring.

Rnd 1 (Right side): Work beginning Popcorn in ring, ch 2, work Popcorn in ring, ch 5, ★ work Popcorn in ring, ch 2, work Popcorn in ring, ch 5; repeat from ★ 2 times **more**; join with slip st to top of beginning Popcorn, finish off: 8 Popcorns.

Note: Loop a short piece of yarn around any stitch to mark last round as **right** side.

Rnd 2: With **right** side facing, join Lt Blue with slip st in first ch-2 sp; work (beginning Popcorn, ch 3, Popcorn) in same sp (corner made), ch 2, 3 dc in next ch-5 sp, ch 2, ★ work (Popcorn, ch 3, Popcorn) in next ch-2 sp, ch 2, 3 dc in next ch-5 sp, ch 2; repeat from ★ around; join with slip st to top of beginning Popcorn, finish off.

Rnd 3: With **right** side facing, join Blue with slip st in any corner ch-3 sp; work (beginning Popcorn, ch 3, Popcorn) in same sp, ch 2, 2 dc in next ch-2 sp, dc in next 3 dc, 2 dc in next ch-2 sp, ch 2, ★ work (Popcorn, ch 3, Popcorn) in next corner ch-3 sp, ch 2, 2 dc in next ch-2 sp, dc in next 3 dc, 2 dc in next ch-2 sp, ch 2; repeat from ★ around; join with slip st to top of beginning Popcorn, finish off.

Rnd 4: With **right** side facing, join White with slip st in any corner ch-3 sp; in same sp work (beginning Popcorn, ch 2, 2 tr, ch 2, Popcorn), ★ † ch 1, work Popcorn in next ch-2 sp, ch 1, work Popcorn in next dc, ch 1, (skip next dc, work Popcorn in next dc, ch 1) 3 times, work Popcorn in next ch-2 sp, ch 1 †, in next corner ch-3 sp work (Popcorn, ch 2, 2 tr, ch 2, Popcorn); repeat from ★ 2 times **more**, then repeat from † to † once; join with slip st to top of beginning Popcorn, finish off.

ASSEMBLY

With White, whipstitch Squares together, forming 9 vertical strips of 12 Squares each *(Fig. 28b, page 142)*, beginning in second tr of first corner and ending in first tr of next corner; then whipstitch strips together in same manner.

Continued on page 14.

ARAN COMFORT

Ideal for snuggling by a blazing fire, this classic Aran design is richly textured with cluster diamonds, cables, and front post stitches. Each panel is worked separately and then joined with easy single crochets.

Finished Size: 47" x 51"

MATERIALS

Worsted Weight Yarn:
50 ounces, (1,420 grams, 3,145 yards)
Crochet hook, size J (6.00 mm) **or** size needed
for gauge

GAUGE: 13 sc and 13 rows = 4"

STITCH GUIDE

CLUSTER
★ YO, insert hook in st indicated, YO and pull up a loop, YO and draw through 2 loops on hook; repeat from ★ 2 times **more**, YO and draw through all 4 loops on hook *(Figs. 9a & b, page 137)*.
FRONT POST DOUBLE CROCHET *(abbreviated FPdc)*
YO, insert hook from **front** to **back** around post of st indicated, YO and pull up a loop *(Fig. 13, page 137)*, (YO and draw through 2 loops on hook) twice.
CABLE
Ch 3 **loosely**, skip next 2 sc on Row 1, sc in next sc, **turn**; sc in next 3 chs, slip st in next sc, **turn**.

DIAMOND PANEL (Make 3)

Ch 20 **loosely**.

Row 1 (Right side)**:** Sc in second ch from hook and in each ch across: 19 sc.

Note: Loop a short piece of yarn around any stitch to mark last row as **right** side and bottom edge.

Row 2: Ch 1, turn; sc in first 9 sc, work Cluster in next sc, sc in last 9 sc.

Row 3: Ch 1, turn; sc in first sc, work FPdc around sc one row **below** next sc, sc in next 15 sts, work FPdc around sc one row **below** next sc, sc in last sc.

Row 4: Ch 1, turn; sc in first 7 sts, work Cluster in next sc, sc in next 3 sc, work Cluster in next sc, sc in last 7 sts.

Row 5: Ch 1, turn; sc in first sc, work FPdc around FPdc one row **below** next sc, sc in next 15 sts, work FPdc around FPdc one row **below** next sc, sc in last sc.

Row 6: Ch 1, turn; sc in first 5 sts, work Cluster in next sc, sc in next 7 sc, work Cluster in next sc, sc in last 5 sts.

Row 7: Ch 1, turn; sc in first sc, work FPdc around FPdc one row **below** next sc, sc in next 15 sts, work FPdc around FPdc one row **below** next sc, sc in last sc.

Row 8: Ch 1, turn; sc in first 7 sts, work Cluster in next sc, sc in next 3 sc, work Cluster in next sc, sc in last 7 sts.

Row 9: Ch 1, turn; sc in first sc, work FPdc around FPdc one row **below** next sc, sc in next 15 sts, work FPdc around FPdc one row **below** next sc, sc in last sc.

Row 10: Ch 1, turn; sc in first 9 sts, work Cluster in next sc, sc in last 9 sts.

Row 11: Ch 1, turn; sc in first sc, work FPdc around FPdc one row **below** next sc, sc in next 15 sts, work FPdc around FPdc one row **below** next sc, sc in last sc.

Rows 12-163: Repeat Rows 4-11, 19 times.
Do **not** finish off.

SC EDGING

Ch 1, working in end of rows, 2 sc in first row, sc in each row across to last row, 2 sc in last row; working in free loops of beginning ch *(Fig. 23b, page 140)*, slip st in next st and in each st across; working in ends of rows, 2 sc in first row, sc in each row across to last row, 2 sc in last row; do **not** finish off: 165 sc along **each** long edge.

CABLE EDGING

Row 1: Ch 1, turn; sc in each sc across.

Row 2: Ch 1, turn; sc in first 2 sc, ★ work Cable, working **behind** Cable, sc in 2 skipped sc; repeat from ★ across to last sc, slip st in sc worked **before** ch-3 of last Cable, sc in last sc: 54 Cables.

Row 3: Ch 1, turn; sc in first sc, skip next slip st, working in **front** of Cables, (2 sc in next sc, sc in next sc, skip next slip st) across, 2 sc in last sc: 165 sc.

Row 4: Ch 1, turn; sc in each sc across; finish off.
Do **not** work Cable Edging on Second Side.

Continued on page 15.

WINTRY DAY

This wintry ripple design resembling snow-covered hills is created with three shades of cool blue. A warming wrap to enjoy after a jaunty afternoon of sledding, it's worked with shell and post stitches.

Finished Size: 48" x 64"

MATERIALS

Worsted Weight Yarn:
Dk Blue - 16½ ounces, (470 grams, 1,085 yards)
Blue - 14 ounces, (400 grams, 920 yards)
Lt Blue - 14 ounces, (400 grams, 920 yards)
Crochet hook, size N (9.00 mm) **or** size needed
for gauge

GAUGE: In pattern, 17 sts (point to point) = 4"

COLOR SEQUENCE

4 rows Dk Blue **(Fig. 24a, page 140)**, 6 rows Blue, 6 rows Lt Blue, ★ 6 rows Dk Blue, 6 rows Blue, 6 rows Lt Blue; repeat from ★ 2 times **more**, 4 rows Dk Blue.

STITCH GUIDE

SHELL
(2 Dc, ch 1, 2 dc) in st or sp indicated.

BACK POST DOUBLE CROCHET DECREASE
(abbreviated BPdc decrease) (uses next 2 sts)
★ YO, insert hook from **back** to **front** around post of **next** st **(Fig. 12, page 137)**, YO and pull up a loop, YO and draw through 2 loops on hook; repeat from ★ once **more**, YO and draw through all 3 loops on hook.

FRONT POST DOUBLE CROCHET
(abbreviated FPdc)
YO, insert hook from **front** to **back** around post of st indicated, YO and pull up a loop **(Fig. 13, page 137)**, (YO and draw through 2 loops on hook) twice.

FRONT POST DOUBLE CROCHET DECREASE
(abbreviated FPdc decrease) (uses next 2 sts)
★ YO, insert hook from **front** to **back** around post of **next** st **(Fig. 12, page 137)**, YO and pull up a loop, YO and draw through 2 loops on hook; repeat from ★ once **more**, YO and draw through all 3 loops on hook.

BACK POST DOUBLE CROCHET
(abbreviated BPdc)
YO, insert hook from **back** to **front** around post of st indicated, YO and pull up a loop **(Fig. 14, page 138)**, (YO and draw through 2 loops on hook) twice.

With Dk Blue, ch 195 **loosely**.

Row 1 (Right side)**:** YO, insert hook in fourth ch from hook, YO and pull up a loop, YO and draw through 2 loops on hook, YO, insert hook in **next** ch, YO and pull up a loop, YO and draw through 2 loops on hook, YO and draw through all 3 loops on hook, dc in next 5 chs, work Shell in next ch, dc in next 5 chs, ★ (YO, insert hook in **next** ch, YO and pull up a loop, YO and draw through 2 loops on hook) 5 times, YO and draw through all 6 loops on hook, dc in next 5 chs, work Shell in next ch, dc in next 5 chs; repeat from ★ across to last 3 chs, (YO, insert hook in **next** ch, YO and pull up a loop, YO and draw through 2 loops on hook) 3 times, YO and draw through all 4 loops on hook: 181 sts and 12 ch-1 sps.

Row 2: Ch 3, turn; work BPdc decrease, work FPdc around next 5 sts, work Shell in next ch-1 sp, work FPdc around next 5 sts, ★ (YO, insert hook from **back** to **front** around post of **next** st, YO and pull up a loop, YO and draw through 2 loops on hook) 5 times, YO and draw through all 6 loops on hook, work FPdc around next 5 sts, work Shell in next ch-1 sp, work FPdc around next 5 sts; repeat from ★ across to last 3 sts, (YO, insert hook from **back** to **front** around post of **next** st, YO and pull up a loop, YO and draw through 2 loops on hook) 3 times, YO and draw through all 4 loops on hook.

Row 3: Ch 3, turn; work FPdc decrease, work BPdc around next 5 sts, work Shell in next ch-1 sp, work BPdc around next 5 sts, ★ (YO, insert hook from **front** to **back** around post of **next** st, YO and pull up a loop, YO and draw through 2 loops on hook) 5 times, YO and draw through all 6 loops on hook, work BPdc around next 5 sts, work Shell in next ch-1 sp, work BPdc around next 5 sts; repeat from ★ across to last 3 sts, (YO, insert hook from **front** to **back** around post of **next** st, YO and pull up a loop, YO and draw through 2 loops on hook) 3 times, YO and draw through all 4 loops on hook.

Row 4: Repeat Row 2.

Continued on page 14.

PATCHWORK STARS

Illuminated with old-fashioned charm, this afghan was inspired by the star motifs found in many antique quilts. Puff stitches create the star outlines as each block is crocheted all in ecru using afghan stitch. The "patches" of color are added later in cross stitch.

Finished Size: 49" x 68"

MATERIALS
Worsted Weight Yarn:
    Ecru - 57 ounces, (1,620 grams, 3,745 yards)
    Yellow - 1/2 ounce, (15 grams, 35 yards)
    Gold - 1 1/2 ounces, (40 grams, 100 yards)
    Lt Blue - 1/2 ounce, (15 grams, 35 yards)
    Blue - 1 1/2 ounces, (40 grams, 100 yards)
    Lt Jade - 1/2 ounce, (15 grams, 35 yards)
    Jade - 1 1/2 ounces, (40 grams, 100 yards)
    Lt Rose - 1/2 ounce, (15 grams, 35 yards)
    Rose - 1 1/2 ounces, (40 grams, 100 yards)
Afghan hook, size J (6.00 mm) **or** size needed
    for gauge
Crochet hook, size H (5.00 mm) **or** size needed
    for gauge
Yarn needle

GAUGE: In Afghan Stitch, 16 sts and 13 rows = 4"
    Each Block = 15 1/4" x 16 1/4"
    Edging, 13 sc = 4"

BLOCK (Make 12)

With Ecru and afghan hook, ch 49 **loosely**.
Rows 1-3: Work 3 rows in Afghan Stitch, following basic instructions, page 139.
Note #1: Loop a short piece of yarn around any stitch to mark last row as **right** side and bottom edge.
Note #2: To work **Puff St**, YO, insert hook in next bar, YO and pull up a loop, (YO, insert hook in **same** bar, YO and pull up a loop) twice, YO and draw through 6 loops on hook, ch 1 to close.
Row 4 - Step 1: Pull up a loop in next 15 bars (16 loops on hook), work Puff St, pull up a loop in next 15 bars, work Puff St, pull up a loop in last 16 bars.
Row 4 - Step 2: Keeping Puff Sts pushed to **right** side of piece, work Step 2 of Afghan Stitch.
Continue to work in Afghan Stitch for a total of 43 rows, working Puff Sts following Chart, page 14.
Work Bind-off Row, page 139.

EDGING

Rnd 1: Transfer remaining loop to crochet hook, ch 1, ★ (sc, ch 2, sc) in first row, sc in end of each row across to last row, (sc, ch 2, sc) in last row; sc in next 3 sts, (skip next st, sc in next 4 sts) 9 times; repeat from ★ once **more**; join with slip st to first sc: 168 sc.
Note: To work **Puff St**, YO, insert hook in st or sp indicated, YO and pull up a loop, (YO, insert hook in **same** st or sp, YO and pull up a loop) twice, YO and draw through all 7 loops on hook *(Fig. 11, page 137)*, ch 1 to close.
Rnd 2: Slip st in first ch-2 sp, pull up loop on hook to measure 1/2", ★ work (Puff St, ch 2, Puff St) in corner ch-2 sp, ch 1, skip next 2 sc, work Puff St in next sc, ch 1, (skip next sc, work Puff St in next sc, ch 1) across to within 2 sc of next corner ch-2 sp; repeat from ★ around; join with slip st to first Puff St: 86 Puff Sts.
Rnd 3: Slip st in first ch-2 sp, ch 1, ★ (2 sc, ch 2, 2 sc) in ch-2 sp, sc in each Puff St and in each ch-1 sp across to next corner ch-2 sp; repeat from ★ around; join with slip st to first sc: 184 sc.
Rnd 4: Slip st in next sc and in first ch-2 sp, pull up loop on hook to measure 1/2", ★ work (Puff St, ch 2, Puff St) in corner ch-2 sp, ch 1, skip next 2 sc, work Puff St in next sc, ch 1, (skip next sc, work Puff St in next sc, ch 1) across to within 2 sc of next corner ch-2 sp; repeat from ★ around; join with slip st to first Puff St: 94 Puff Sts.
Rnd 5: Slip st in first ch-2 sp, ch 1, ★ (sc, ch 2, sc) in ch-2 sp, sc in each Puff St and in each ch-1 sp across to next corner ch-2 sp; repeat from ★ around; join with slip st to first sc, finish off: 192 sc.

EMBROIDERY

Add Cross Stitch *(Fig. 21, page 139)* to all Blocks following Chart, page 14.

ASSEMBLY

Using Ecru, whipstitch Blocks together, forming 3 vertical strips of 4 Blocks each *(Fig. 28b, page 142)*, beginning in second ch of first corner and ending in first ch of next corner; then whipstitch strips together in same manner.

Continued on page 14.

PATCHWORK STARS Continued from page 12.

BORDER

Rnd 1: With **right** side facing and using crochet hook, join Ecru with slip st in any corner ch-2 sp; pull up loop on hook to measure ¹/₂", ★ work (Puff St, ch 2, Puff St) in corner ch-2 sp, ch 1, [(skip next sc, work Puff St in next sc, ch 1) across to within one sc of next joining, skip next sc and next ch-1 sp, work Puff St in next joining, ch 1] across to last Block, skip next sc, (work Puff St in next sc, ch 1, skip next sc) across to next corner ch-2 sp; repeat from ★ around; join with slip st to first Puff St.
Rnds 2-4: Work same as Rnds 3-5 of Block Edging, page 12.

Holding five strands of Ecru together, add fringe evenly across short edges of Afghan *(Figs. 29a & c, page 142)*.

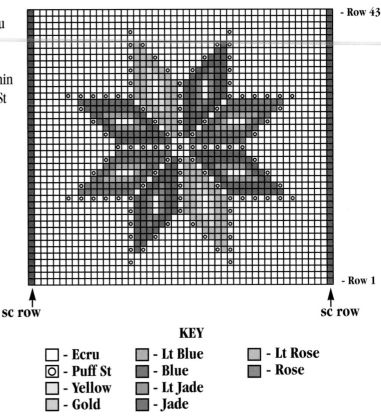

- Row 43

- Row 1

sc row   sc row

KEY

☐ - Ecru	▨ - Lt Blue	▨ - Lt Rose
⊡ - Puff St	▨ - Blue	▨ - Rose
☐ - Yellow	▨ - Lt Jade	
☐ - Gold	▨ - Jade	

FROSTY FLOWERS Continued from page 6.

EDGING

With **right** side facing, join White with slip st in sp **between** any corner 2-tr group *(Fig. 26, page 141)*; work beginning Popcorn in same sp, ch 2, work Popcorn in next ch-2 sp, ch 1, ★ (work Popcorn in next Popcorn, ch 1) 8 times, † work Popcorn in Front Loop Only of next tr *(Fig. 22, page 140)*, ch 1, skip joining, work Popcorn in Front Loop Only of next tr, ch 1, (work Popcorn in next Popcorn, ch 1) 8 times †, repeat from † to † across to next corner ch-2 sp, work Popcorn in corner ch-2 sp, ch 2, skip next tr, work Popcorn in sp **before** next tr, ch 2, work Popcorn in next ch-2 sp, ch 1; repeat from ★ 2 times **more**, (work Popcorn in next Popcorn, ch 1) 8 times, repeat from † to † across to next corner ch-2 sp, work Popcorn in corner ch-2 sp, ch 2; join with slip st to top of beginning Popcorn, finish off.

WINTRY DAY Continued from page 10.

Row 5: Ch 3, turn; [YO, insert hook in Front Loop Only *(Fig. 22, page 140)* of **next** st, YO and pull up a loop, YO and draw through 2 loops on hook] twice, YO and draw through all 3 loops on hook, dc in Back Loop Only of next 5 sts, work Shell in next ch-1 sp, dc in Back Loop Only of next 5 sts, ★ (YO, insert hook in Front Loop Only of **next** st, YO and pull up a loop, YO and draw through 2 loops on hook) 5 times, YO and draw through all 6 loops on hook, dc in Back Loop Only of next 5 sts, work Shell in next ch-1 sp, dc in Back Loop Only of next 5 sts; repeat from ★ across to last 3 sts, (YO, insert hook in Front Loop Only of **next** st, YO and pull up a loop, YO and draw through 2 loops on hook) 3 times, YO and draw through all 4 loops on hook.
Rows 6-10: Repeat Rows 2 and 3 twice, then repeat Row 2 once **more**.
Rows 11-74: Repeat Rows 5-10, 10 times; then repeat Rows 5-8 once **more**.
Finish off.

TEXTURED PANEL (Make 2)

Ch 32 **loosely**.

Row 1 (Right side)**:** Sc in second ch from hook and in each ch across: 31 sc.

Note: Mark last row as **right** side and bottom edge.

Row 2: Ch 1, turn; sc in first 4 sc, tr in next sc, (sc in next sc, tr in next sc) 11 times, sc in last 4 sc: 31 sts.

Row 3: Ch 1, turn; sc in first sc, work FPdc around sc one row **below** next sc, sc in next 27 sts, work FPdc around sc one row **below** next sc, sc in last sc.

Row 4: Ch 1, turn; sc in first 4 sts, tr in next sc, (sc in next sc, tr in next sc) 11 times, sc in last 4 sts.

Row 5: Ch 1, turn; sc in first sc, work FPdc around FPdc one row **below** next sc, sc in next 27 sts, work FPdc around FPdc one row **below** next sc, sc in last sc.

Rows 6-163: Repeat Rows 4 and 5, 79 times.

Do **not** finish off.

SC EDGING

Ch 1, working in end of rows, 2 sc in first row, sc in each row across to last row, 2 sc in last row; working in free loops of beginning ch, slip st in next st and in each st across; working in end of rows, 2 sc in first row, sc in each row across to last row, 2 sc in last row; do **not** finish off: 165 sc along **each** long edge.

CABLE EDGING

Row 1: Ch 1, turn; sc in each sc across.

Row 2: Ch 1, turn; sc in first 2 sc, ★ work Cable, working **behind** Cable, sc in 2 skipped sc; repeat from ★ across to last sc, slip st in sc worked **before** ch-3 of last Cable, sc in last sc: 54 Cables.

Row 3: Ch 1, turn; sc in first sc, skip next slip st, working in **front** of Cables, (2 sc in next sc, sc in next sc, skip next slip st) across, 2 sc in last sc: 165 sc.

Row 4: Ch 1, turn; sc in each sc across; finish off.

Do **not** work Cable Edging on Second Side.

JOINING

Note: Beginning and ending with **Diamond Panel**, alternate Diamond and Textured Panels as you join.

Place two panels with **right** sides and long edges together, and bottom edges at same end. Working through sc of **both** Panels, join yarn with slip st in first sc; ch 1, sc in each sc across; finish off.

Repeat to join remaining Panels.

LAST CABLE EDGING

Row 1: With **wrong** side facing and working along long edge of Diamond Panel **without** Cable Edging, join yarn with slip st in first sc; ch 1, sc in each sc across.

Row 2: Ch 1, turn; sc in first 2 sc, ★ work Cable, working **behind** Cable, sc in 2 skipped sc; repeat from ★ across to last sc, slip st in sc worked **before** ch-3 of last Cable, sc in last sc: 54 Cables.

Row 3: Ch 1, turn; sc in first sc, skip next slip st, working in **front** of Cables, (2 sc in next sc, sc in next sc, skip next slip st) across, 2 sc in last sc: 165 sc.

Row 4: Ch 1, turn; sc in each sc across; finish off.

Holding four strands of yarn together, add fringe across short edges of Afghan *(Figs. 29a & c, page 142)*.

COZY LOG CABIN

Inspired by Log Cabin quilts, this colorful afghan is a Presidents' Day tribute to Abraham Lincoln and his humble beginnings. Each block is simple to make in single crochet by starting with a red center square and adding a succession of colored "strips."

Finished Size: 42" x 61"

MATERIALS

Worsted Weight Yarn:
Red - 2 ounces,
(60 grams, 125 yards)
Lt Green - 3 ounces,
(90 grams, 190 yards)
Brown - 4 ounces,
(110 grams, 250 yards)
Natural - 5 ounces,
(140 grams, 315 yards)
Dk Red - 7 ounces,
(200 grams, 440 yards)
Rose - 8 ounces,
(230 grams, 505 yards)
Dk Green - 10 ounces,
(280 grams, 630 yards)
Crochet hook, size J (6.00 mm) **or** size needed for gauge
Yarn needle

GAUGE: 12 sc and 16 rows = 4"
Each Square = 9¹/₂" x 9¹/₂"

SQUARE (Make 24)

With Red, ch 6 **loosely**.

Row 1 (Right side)**:** Sc in second ch from hook and in each ch across: 5 sc.

Note: Loop a short piece of yarn around any stitch to mark last row as **right** side.

Rows 2-6: Ch 1, turn; sc in each sc across, changing to Lt Green in last sc on Row 6 **(Fig. 24a, page 140)**.

Rows 7-11: Ch 1, turn; sc in each sc across.

Row 12: Ch 1, working in end of rows, sc in first 2 rows, skip next row, sc in next 5 rows, skip next row, sc in last 2 rows: 9 sc.

Rows 13-16: Ch 1, turn; sc in each sc across, changing to Brown in last sc worked on Row 16.

Row 17: Ch 1, sc in end of first 2 rows, skip next row, sc in end of next 2 rows, sc in free loop of next 5 chs **(Fig. 23b, page 140)**: 9 sc.

Rows 18-21: Ch 1, turn; sc in each sc across.

Row 22: Ch 1, working in end of rows, sc in next 2 rows, skip next row, sc in next 5 rows, (skip next row, sc in next 3 rows) twice: 13 sc.

Rows 23-26: Ch 1, turn; sc in each sc across, changing to Natural in last sc worked on Row 26.

Row 27: Ch 1, sc in end of next 2 rows, skip next row, sc in end of next 2 rows, sc in next 5 sc, sc in end of next 2 rows, skip next row, sc in end of next 2 rows: 13 sc.

Rows 28-31: Ch 1, turn; sc in each sc across.

Row 32: Ch 1, sc in end of next 2 rows, skip next row, sc in end of next 2 rows, sc in next 9 sc, sc in end of next 2 rows, skip next row, sc in end of next 2 rows: 17 sc.

Rows 33-36: Ch 1, turn; sc in each sc across, changing to Dk Red in last sc worked on Row 36.

Row 37: Repeat Row 32.

Rows 38-41: Ch 1, turn; sc in each sc across.

Row 42: Ch 1, sc in end of next 2 rows, skip next row, sc in end of next 2 rows, sc in next 13 sc, sc in end of next 2 rows, skip next row, sc in end of next 2 rows: 21 sc.

Rows 43-46: Ch 1, turn; sc in each sc across, changing to Rose in last sc worked on Row 46.

Continued on page 25.

february

17

LOVE SONGS

*With its dimensional floral motifs, this lovely afghan offers a note
of romance for Valentine's Day. The frilly squares, created with clusters
and chain spaces, are edged with lacy V-stitch scallops. To add the flower
petals, simply work single crochets into the first round of each square.*

Finished Size: 49" x 62"

MATERIALS

Worsted Weight Yarn:
  White - 13 ounces, (370 grams, 855 yards)
  Lt Rose - 12 ounces, (340 grams, 790 yards)
  Rose - 11 ounces, (310 grams, 725 yards)
  Green - 6 ounces, (170 grams, 395 yards)
Crochet hook, size I (5.50 mm) **or** size needed
  for gauge
Yarn needle

GAUGE: Each Square = 6¾"

STITCH GUIDE

BEGINNING CLUSTER
Ch 2, ★ YO, insert hook in **same** sp, YO and pull up a
loop, YO and draw through 2 loops on hook; repeat from
★ 2 times **more**, YO and draw through all 4 loops on hook
(Figs. 9a & b, page 137).

CLUSTER
★ YO, insert hook in sp indicated, YO and pull up a loop,
YO and draw through 2 loops on hook; repeat from ★
3 times **more**, YO and draw through all 5 loops on hook.

V-ST
(Dc, ch 1, dc) in next dc.

SQUARE (Make 63)

With Green, ch 6; join with slip st to form a ring.

Rnd 1 (Right side): Ch 5 **(counts as first dc plus ch 2)**, (dc
in ring, ch 2) 7 times; join with slip st to third ch of beginning
ch-5: 8 ch-2 sps.

Note: Loop a short piece of yarn around any stitch to mark last
round as **right** side.

Rnd 2: Slip st in first ch-2 sp, work beginning Cluster, ch 5,
(work Cluster in next ch-2 sp, ch 5) around; join with slip st to
top of beginning Cluster, finish off.

Rnd 3: With **right** side facing, join White with slip st in top of
any Cluster; ch 1, sc in same st, ch 2, working around next
ch-5 loop, dc in next dc on Rnd 1, ★ ch 2, sc in next Cluster,
ch 2, working around next ch-5 loop, dc in next dc on Rnd 1;
repeat from ★ around, ch 1, sc in first sc to form last sp.

Rnd 4: Ch 1, sc in same sp, (ch 3, sc in next ch-2 sp) around,
ch 1, hdc in first sc to form last sp: 16 sps.

Rnd 5: Ch 3 **(counts as first dc, now and throughout)**, dc
in same sp, ch 2, sc in next ch-3 sp, (ch 3, sc in next ch-3 sp)
twice, ch 2, ★ (2 dc, ch 2, 2 dc) in next ch-3 sp (corner
made), ch 2, sc in next ch-3 sp, (ch 3, sc in next ch-3 sp) twice,
ch 2; repeat from ★ around, 2 dc in same sp as first dc, hdc in
first dc to form last sp.

Rnd 6: Ch 3, (dc, ch 2, 2 dc) in same sp, ch 2, sc in next
ch-2 sp, (ch 3, sc in next sp) 3 times, ch 2, ★ (2 dc, ch 2, 2 dc)
in next corner ch-2 sp, ch 2, sc in next ch-2 sp, (ch 3, sc in next
sp) 3 times, ch 2; repeat from ★ around; join with slip st to first
dc, finish off.

Rnd 7: With **right** side facing, join Rose with slip st in any
corner ch-2 sp; ch 3, (dc, ch 2, 2 dc) in same sp, 2 dc in next
ch-2 sp, (dc in next sc, 2 dc in next sp) 4 times, ★ (2 dc, ch 2,
2 dc) in next corner ch-2 sp, 2 dc in next ch-2 sp, (dc in next
sc, 2 dc in next sp) 4 times; repeat from ★ around; join with
slip st to first dc, finish off: 72 dc.

Rnd 8: With **right** side facing, join Lt Rose with slip st in any
corner ch-2 sp; ch 3, (dc, ch 2, 2 dc) in same sp, skip next dc,
work V-St, (skip next 2 dc, work V-St) 5 times, skip next dc,
★ (2 dc, ch 2, 2 dc) in next corner ch-2 sp, skip next dc, work
V-St, (skip next 2 dc, work V-St) 5 times, skip next dc; repeat
from ★ around; join with slip st to first dc, finish off.

FLOWER

Rnd 1: With **right** side facing and working around post of sts
on Rnd 1 of Square *(Fig. 12, page 137)*, join Lt Rose with
slip st around any dc; ch 1, (sc, ch 5, sc) around same st, ch 5,
★ (sc, ch 5, sc) around next dc, ch 5; repeat from ★ around;
join with slip st to first sc, finish off.

Rnd 2: With **right** side facing and working around post of
same sts on Rnd 1 of Square and **behind** sts of previous rnd,
join Rose with slip st around any dc; ch 1, sc around same st,
ch 7, (sc around next dc, ch 7) around; join with slip st to first
sc, finish off.

Continued on page 25.

HUGS & KISSES

Wrap baby in hand-stitched hugs and kisses — they're worked right into this adorable afghan! Accented with satin ribbon, the pattern of airy X's and O's is made with effortless double crochets and chain spaces using soft, cuddly sport weight baby yarn.

Finished Size: 40" x 51"

MATERIALS

Sport Weight Baby Yarn:
   20 ounces, (570 grams, 2,150 yards)
Crochet hook, size F (3.75 mm) **or** size needed
   for gauge
9 yards of ¼" wide ribbon
Yarn needle
Sewing needle and thread

GAUGE: 18 sts and 9 rows = 4"

PANEL A (Make 4)

Ch 25 **loosely**.

Row 1 (Right side): Dc in fourth ch from hook and in each ch across: 23 sts.

Note: Loop a short piece of yarn around any stitch to mark last row as **right** side and bottom edge.

Row 2: Ch 3 **(counts as first dc, now and throughout)**, turn; dc in next dc and in each st across.

Row 3: Ch 3, turn; dc in next 4 dc, ch 1, skip next dc, dc in next 11 dc, ch 1, skip next dc, dc in last 5 dc.

Row 4: Ch 3, turn; dc in next 4 dc, dc in next ch-1 sp and in next dc, ch 1, skip next dc, dc in next 7 dc, ch 1, skip next dc, dc in next dc and in next ch-1 sp, dc in last 5 dc.

Row 5: Ch 3, turn; dc in next 6 dc, dc in next ch-1 sp and in next dc, ch 1, skip next dc, dc in next 3 dc, ch 1, skip next dc, dc in next dc and in next ch-1 sp, dc in last 7 dc.

Row 6: Ch 3, turn; dc in next 8 dc, dc in next ch-1 sp and in next dc, ch 1, skip next dc, dc in next dc and in next ch-1 sp, dc in last 9 dc.

Row 7: Ch 3, turn; dc in next 8 dc, ch 1, skip next dc, dc in next dc, dc in next ch-1 sp and in next dc, ch 1, skip next dc, dc in last 9 dc.

Row 8: Ch 3, turn; dc in next 6 dc, ch 1, skip next dc, dc in next dc, dc in next ch-1 sp and in next 3 dc, dc in next ch-1 sp and in next dc, ch 1, skip next dc, dc in last 7 dc.

Row 9: Ch 3, turn; dc in next 4 dc, ch 1, skip next dc, dc in next dc and in next ch-1 sp, dc in next 7 dc, dc in next ch-1 sp and in next dc, ch 1, skip next dc, dc in last 5 dc.

Row 10: Ch 3, turn; dc in next dc and in each dc and ch-1 sp across: 23 dc.

Rows 11 and 12: Ch 3, turn; dc in next dc and in each dc across.

Row 13: Ch 3, turn; dc in next 8 dc, ch 1, (skip next dc, dc in next dc, ch 1) twice, skip next dc, dc in last 9 dc.

Row 14: Ch 3, turn; dc in next 6 dc, ch 1, skip next dc, dc in next dc, (dc in next ch-1 sp, dc in next dc) 3 times, ch 1, skip next dc, dc in last 7 dc.

Row 15: Ch 3, turn; dc in next 4 dc, ch 1, skip next dc, dc in next dc and in next ch-1 sp, dc in next 7 dc, dc in next ch-1 sp and in next dc, ch 1, skip next dc, dc in last 5 dc.

Rows 16 and 17: Ch 3, turn; dc in next 4 dc, ch 1, skip next ch-1 sp, dc in next 11 dc, ch 1, skip next ch-1 sp, dc in last 5 dc.

Row 18: Ch 3, turn; dc in next 4 dc, dc in next ch-1 sp and in next dc, ch 1, skip next dc, dc in next 7 dc, ch 1, skip next dc, dc in next dc and in next ch-1 sp, dc in last 5 dc.

Row 19: Ch 3, turn; dc in next 6 dc, dc in next ch-1 sp and in next dc, (ch 1, skip next dc, dc in next dc) 3 times, dc in next ch-1 sp, dc in last 7 dc.

Row 20: Ch 3, turn; dc in next dc and in each dc and ch-1 sp across.

Rows 21 and 22: Ch 3, turn; dc in next dc and in each dc across.

Rows 23-111: Repeat Rows 3-22, 4 times, then repeat Rows 3-11 once **more**.
Finish off.

PANEL B (Make 3)

Ch 25 **loosely**.

Row 1 (Right side): Dc in fourth ch from hook and in each ch across: 23 sts.

Note: Mark last row as **right** side and bottom edge.

Row 2: Ch 3, turn; dc in next dc and in each st across.

Rows 3-12: Work same as Panel A, Rows 13-22.

Rows 13-111: Work same as Panel A, Rows 3-22, 4 times, then repeat Rows 3-21 once **more**.
Finish off.

Continued on page 24.

SWEET HEARTS

You'll have sweet dreams of your valentine when you nap beneath this afghan featuring a patchwork of granny squares. Our handy placement diagram makes it easy to assemble the colored squares in the shape of large hearts!

Finished Size: 57" x 71"

MATERIALS

Worsted Weight Yarn:
White - 37 ounces, (1,050 grams, 2,095 yards)
Variegated - 19 ounces, (540 grams, 1,075 yards)
Pink - 13 ounces, (370 grams, 735 yards)
Blue - 6 ounces, (170 grams, 340 yards)
Crochet hook, size I (5.50 mm) **or** size needed for gauge
Yarn needle

GAUGE: Each Square = 3½"

ONE COLOR SQUARE

Make 225 as follows:
With White, make 141.
With Variegated, make 42.
With Pink, make 21.
With Blue, make 21.
Ch 4; join with slip st to form a ring.
Rnd 1 (Right side): Ch 3 **(counts as first dc, now and throughout)**, 2 dc in ring, ch 2, (3 dc in ring, ch 2) 3 times; join with slip st to first dc: 12 dc.
Note: Loop a short piece of yarn around any stitch to mark last round as **right** side.
Rnd 2: Turn; slip st in first ch-2 sp, ch 3, 2 dc in same sp, ch 1, ★ (3 dc, ch 2, 3 dc) in next ch-2 sp, ch 1; repeat from ★ 2 times **more**, 3 dc in same sp as first dc, ch 2; join with slip st to first dc: 24 dc.
Rnd 3: Turn; slip st in first ch-2 sp, ch 3, 2 dc in same sp, ch 1, 3 dc in next ch-1 sp, ch 1, ★ (3 dc, ch 2, 3 dc) in next ch-2 sp, ch 1, 3 dc in next ch-1 sp, ch 1; repeat from ★ 2 times **more**, 3 dc in same sp as first dc, ch 2; join with slip st to first dc, finish off: 36 dc.

TWO COLORED SQUARE

Make 60 as follows:
With White and Variegated, make 30.
With White and Pink, make 15.
With White and Blue, make 15.
With White, ch 4; join with slip st to form a ring.
Note: When changing colors *(Fig. 24a, page 140)*, keep unused color to **wrong** side of Square. Do **not** cut yarn unless instructed.
Rnd 1 (Right side): Ch 3 **(counts as first dc, now and throughout)**, 2 dc in ring, ch 2, 3 dc in ring changing to next color in last dc, ch 2, (3 dc in ring, ch 2) twice; join with slip st to first dc: 12 dc.
Note: Mark last round as **right** side.
Rnd 2: Turn; slip st in first ch-2 sp, ch 3, 2 dc in same sp, ch 1, (3 dc, ch 2, 3 dc) in next ch-2 sp, ch 1, 3 dc in next ch-2 sp changing to White in last dc, ch 2, 3 dc in same sp, ch 1, (3 dc, ch 2, 3 dc) in next ch-2 sp, ch 1, 3 dc in same sp as first dc, ch 2; join with slip st to first dc: 24 dc.
Rnd 3: Turn; slip st in first ch-2 sp, ch 3, 2 dc in same sp, ch 1, 3 dc in next ch-1 sp, ch 1, (3 dc, ch 2, 3 dc) in next ch-2 sp, (ch 1, 3 dc in next ch-sp) twice changing to next color in last dc, cut White, ch 2, 3 dc in same sp as last dc, ch 1, 3 dc in next ch-1 sp, ch 1, (3 dc, ch 2, 3 dc) in next ch-2 sp, ch 1, 3 dc in next ch-1 sp, ch 1, 3 dc in same sp as first dc, ch 2; join with slip st to first dc, finish off: 36 dc.

ASSEMBLY

With matching color and using Placement Diagram as a guide, page 24, whipstitch Squares together, forming 15 vertical strips of 19 Squares each *(Fig. 28a, page 142)*, beginning in second ch of first corner ch-2 and ending in first ch of next corner ch-2; then whipstitch strips together in same manner.

Continued on page 24.

SWEET HEARTS Continued from page 22.

EDGING

Note: To work **V-St**, (dc, ch 1, dc) in sp indicated.

Rnd 1: With **right** side facing, join Pink with slip st in any corner ch-2 sp; ch 4 **(counts as first dc plus ch 1, now and throughout)**, (dc, ch 2, work V-St) in same sp, ch 1, (work V-St in next ch-sp, ch 1) across to next corner ch-2 sp, ★ work (V-St, ch 2, V-St) in corner ch-2 sp, ch 1, (work V-St in next ch-sp, ch 1) across to next corner ch-2 sp; repeat from ★ around; join with slip st to first dc: 272 V-Sts.

Rnds 2 and 3: Slip st across to first ch-2 sp, ch 4, (dc, ch 2, work V-St) in same sp, ch 1, skip next V-St, (work V-St in next ch-1 sp, ch 1, skip next V-St) across to next corner ch-2 sp, ★ work (V-St, ch 2, V-St) in corner ch-2 sp, ch 1, skip next V-St, (work V-St in next ch-1 sp, ch 1, skip next V-St) across to next corner ch-2 sp; repeat from ★ around; join with slip st to first dc: 280 V-Sts.

Rnd 4: Slip st across to first ch-2 sp, ch 3, (2 dc, ch 2, 3 dc) in same sp, ch 1, skip next V-St, sc in next ch-1 sp, ch 1, skip next V-St, ★ (3 dc, ch 2, 3 dc) in next ch-sp, ch 1, skip next V-St, sc in next ch-1 sp, ch 1, skip next V-St; repeat from ★ around; join with slip st to first dc, finish off.

PLACEMENT DIAGRAM

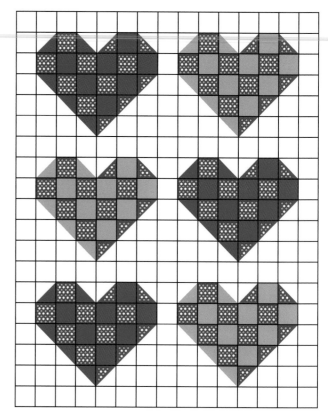

HUGS & KISSES Continued from page 20.

ASSEMBLY

Arrange Panels in the following order: Panel A, (Panel B, Panel A) 3 times.

With **wrong** sides together and beginning at bottom edge, join yarn with slip st in bottom of first row on top panel; ch 2, slip st in bottom of first row on next panel, (ch 2, sc in end of first row on next panel) twice, (ch 2, sc in end of next row on next panel) across, (ch 2, slip st in top of last row on next panel) twice; finish off.

Join remaining Panels in same manner.

EDGING

Rnd 1: With **right** side facing, join yarn with slip st in any dc; ch 1, sc evenly around working 3 sc in each corner; join with slip st to first sc.

Rnd 2: Ch 1, sc in each sc around working 3 sc in each corner sc; join with slip st to first sc, finish off.

RIBBON

Starting at bottom of afghan, loosely weave a ribbon through each joining; tack on **wrong** side at each end.

COZY LOG CABIN Continued from page 16.

Row 47: Ch 1, sc in end of next 2 rows, skip next row, sc in end of next 2 rows, sc in next 13 sc, sc in end of next 2 rows, skip next row, sc in end of next 2 rows: 21 sc.

Rows 48-51: Ch 1, turn; sc in each sc across.

Row 52: Ch 1, sc in end of next 2 rows, skip next row, sc in end of next 2 rows, sc in next 17 sc, sc in end of next 2 rows, skip next row, sc in end of next 2 rows: 25 sc.

Rows 53-56: Ch 1, turn; sc in each sc across, changing to Dk Green in last sc worked on Row 56.

Row 57: Repeat Row 52.

Rows 58-61: Ch 1, turn; sc in each sc across.

Row 62: Ch 1, sc in end of next 2 rows, skip next row, sc in end of next 2 rows, sc in next 21 sc, sc in end of next 2 rows, skip next row, sc in end of next 2 rows: 29 sc.

Rows 63-66: Ch 1, turn; sc in each sc across.
Finish off.

ASSEMBLY

Using Placement Chart as a guide, with **wrong** sides together and matching colors, whipstitch Squares together, forming 4 vertical strips of 6 Squares each *(Fig. 28a, page 142)*; then whipstitch strips in same manner.

EDGING

Rnd 1: With **right** side facing, join Rose with slip st in any corner; ch 1, ★ (sc, ch 1, sc) in corner, work 28 sc evenly spaced across first Square, work 29 sc evenly spaced along each Square across to last Square, work 28 sc evenly spaced across last Square; repeat from ★ around; join with slip st to first sc, finish off.

Note: Work next 8 rnds in the following Color Sequence: Dk Green, Rose, Dk Green, Dk Red, Natural, Brown, Lt Green, Red.

Rnd 2: With **wrong** side facing, join next color with slip st in any sc; ch 1, sc in each sc around working (sc, ch 1, sc) in each corner ch-1 sp; join with slip st to first sc, finish off.

Rnd 3: With **right** side facing, join next color with slip st in any sc; ch 1, sc in each sc around working (sc, ch 1, sc) in each corner ch-1 sp; join with slip st to first sc, finish off.

Rnds 4-9: Repeat Rnds 2 and 3, 3 times.

PLACEMENT CHART

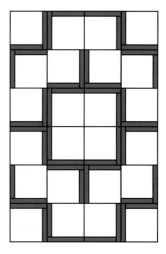

LOVE SONGS Continued from page 18.

ASSEMBLY

With Lt Rose, whipstitch Squares together, forming 7 vertical strips of 9 Squares each *(Fig. 28b, page 142)*, beginning in second ch of first corner ch-2 and ending in first ch of next corner ch-2; then whipstitch strips together in same manner.

EDGING

With **right** side facing, join Rose with slip st in any corner ch-2 sp; ch 1, in same sp work (sc, dc, sc, ch 3, sc, dc, sc), ★ skip next dc, (sc, dc, sc) in sp **before** next dc *(Fig. 26, page 141)*, (sc, dc, sc) in each of next 6 ch-1 sps, skip next 2 dc, (sc, dc, sc) in sp **before** next dc, † (sc, dc, sc) in next joining, skip next dc, (sc, dc, sc) in sp **before** next dc, (sc, dc, sc) in each of next 6 ch-1 sps, skip next 2 dc, (sc, dc, sc) in sp **before** next dc †, repeat from † to † across to next corner ch-2 sp, in corner ch-2 sp work (sc, dc, sc, ch 3, sc, dc, sc); repeat from ★ 2 times **more**, skip next dc, (sc, dc, sc) in sp **before** next dc, (sc, dc, sc) in each of next 6 ch-1 sps, skip next 2 dc, (sc, dc, sc) in sp **before** next dc, repeat from † to † across; join with slip st to first sc, finish off.

COUNTRY PLAID

This home-style afghan works up in a jiffy to commemorate National Craft Month. Each created in just two rounds, the tiny granny squares are joined as you go, forming a handsome plaid pattern.

Finished Size: 52" x 63"

MATERIALS
Worsted Weight Yarn:
Blue - 25½ ounces,
(720 grams, 1,490 yards)
Ecru - 25½ ounces,
(720 grams, 1,490 yards)
Lt Blue - 16½ ounces,
(470 grams, 960 yards)
Crochet hook, size H (5.00 mm) **or** size needed for gauge

GAUGE: Each Square = 2¼"

FIRST SQUARE

With Ecru, ch 4; join with slip st to form a ring.
Rnd 1 (Right side)**:** Ch 3 **(counts as first dc, now and throughout)**, 2 dc in ring, (ch 2, 3 dc in ring) 3 times, hdc in first dc to form last ch-2 sp: 4 ch-2 sps.
Note: Loop a short piece of yarn around any stitch to mark last round as **right** side.
Rnd 2: Ch 3, (2 dc, ch 2, 3 dc) in same sp, ch 1, ★ (3 dc, ch 2, 3 dc) in next ch-2 sp, ch 1; repeat from ★ around; join with slip st to first dc, finish off: 8 sps.

ADDITIONAL SQUARES

Following Placement Chart, page 37, make Squares using color indicated.
Ch 4; join with slip st to form a ring.
Rnd 1: Work same as First Square.
Note: Mark last round as **right** side.
Rnd 2: Work One or Two Side Joining *(Fig. 25, page 140)*.

ONE SIDE JOINING

Ch 3, (2 dc, ch 2, 3 dc) in same sp, ch 1, (3 dc, ch 2, 3 dc) in next ch-2 sp, ch 1, 3 dc in next ch-2 sp, ch 1, holding Squares with **wrong** sides together, slip st in corner sp on **adjacent Square**, ch 1, 3 dc in same ch-2 sp on **new Square**, ch 1, slip st in next ch-1 sp on **adjacent Square**, 3 dc in next ch-2 sp on **new Square**, ch 1, slip st in next corner sp on **adjacent Square**, ch 1, 3 dc in same ch-2 sp on **new Square**, ch 1; join with slip st to first dc, finish off.

TWO SIDE JOINING

Ch 3, (2 dc, ch 2, 3 dc) in same sp, ch 1, 3 dc in next ch-2 sp, ch 1, holding Squares with **wrong** sides together, slip st in corner sp on **adjacent Square**, ch 1, 3 dc in same ch-2 sp on **new Square**, ch 1, slip st in next ch-1 sp on **adjacent Square**, 3 dc in next ch-2 sp on **new Square**, ch 1, (slip st in next corner sp on **adjacent Square**, ch 1) twice, 3 dc in same ch-2 sp on **new Square**, ch 1, slip st in next ch-1 sp on **adjacent Square**, 3 dc in next ch-2 sp on **new Square**, ch 1, slip st in next corner sp on **adjacent Square**, ch 1, 3 dc in same ch-2 sp on **new Square**, ch 1; join with slip st to first dc, finish off.

Holding two strands of corresponding color together, add fringe evenly around entire Afghan *(Figs. 29a & c, page 142)*.

BABY'S RAINBOW GRANNY

All the colors in a baby's rainbow — soft yellow, blue, green, and pink — are found at the heart of the delicate motifs on this afghan. The simple three-round granny squares are whipstitched together and finished with a ruffled edging and satin bows.

Finished Size: 37" x 44"

MATERIALS

Sport Weight Yarn:
 White - 12 ounces, (340 grams, 1,135 yards)
 Pink - 1¼ ounces, (40 grams, 120 yards)
 Green - 1¼ ounces, (40 grams, 120 yards)
 Yellow - 1¼ ounces, (40 grams, 120 yards)
 Blue - 1¼ ounces, (40 grams, 120 yards)
 Crochet hook, size F (3.75 mm) **or** size needed
  for gauge
 7 yards of ³/₈" wide ribbon
 Yarn needle

GAUGE: Each Square = 3¼"

SQUARE (Make 120)

Note: For Rnd 1, make 30 Squares with **each** of the following colors: Pink, Green, Yellow, Blue.

Rnd 1 (Right side)**:** With first color, ch 4, 2 dc in fourth ch from hook, ch 3, (3 dc in same st, ch 3) 3 times; join with slip st to top of beginning ch, finish off.

Note: Loop a short piece of yarn around any stitch to mark last round as **right** side.

Rnd 2: With **right** side facing, join White with slip st in any ch-3 sp; ch 3 **(counts as first dc, now and throughout)**, (2 dc, ch 3, 3 dc) in same sp, ch 1, ★ (3 dc, ch 3, 3 dc) in next ch-3 sp, ch 1; repeat from ★ around; join with slip st to first dc: 24 dc.

Rnd 3: Ch 4, skip next dc, dc in next dc, ch 1, (dc, ch 3, dc) in next ch-3 sp, ch 1, ★ dc in next dc, ch 1, skip next dc, (dc in next dc, ch 1) twice, skip next dc, dc in next dc, ch 1, (dc, ch 3, dc) in next ch-3 sp, ch 1; repeat from ★ 2 times **more**, dc in next dc, ch 1, skip next dc, dc in next dc, ch 1; join with slip st to third ch of beginning ch-4, finish off.

ASSEMBLY

With White and using Placement Diagram as a guide, whipstitch Squares together forming 10 vertical strips of 12 Squares each *(Fig. 28a, page 142)*, beginning in center ch of first corner and ending in center ch of next corner; then whipstitch strips together in same manner.

PLACEMENT DIAGRAM

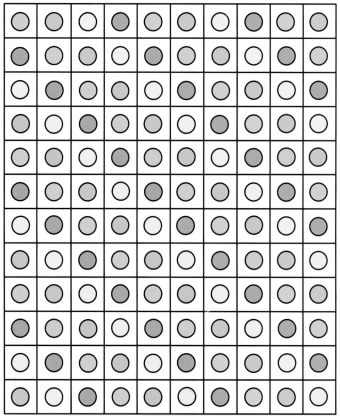

EDGING

Rnd 1: With **right** side facing, join White with sc in any ch-3 sp *(see Joining With Sc, page 140)*; ch 3, sc in same sp, ★ † [(sc in next dc, ch 1) 6 times, sc in next joining, ch 1] across to within 6 dc of next ch-3 sp, sc in next dc, (ch 1, sc in next dc) 5 times †, (sc, ch 3, sc) in next ch-3 sp; repeat from ★ 2 times **more**, then repeat from † to † once; join with slip st to first sc.

Continued on page 38.

TULIP KISSES

*This garden of tulips is a warm greeting for the first days of spring.
Each strip features a tidy row of pink and green tulips against a
field of ecru. Created using one color at a time, the blossoms develop
by working in front of and behind the stitches in previous rows.*

Finished Size: 48½" x 66"

MATERIALS
Worsted Weight Yarn:
    Ecru - 36 ounces, (1,020 grams, 2,365 yards)
    Green - 10 ounces, (280 grams, 655 yards)
    Pink - 8 ounces, (230 grams, 525 yards)
Crochet hook, size I (5.50 mm) **or** size needed
    for gauge
Yarn needle

GAUGE: 14 sc = 4" and 16 rows = 4½"
        Each Strip = 6" wide

STRIP (Make 11)
FIRST SIDE
With Ecru, ch 170 **loosely**.

Row 1 (Right side): Sc in second ch from hook and in each ch across changing to Green in last sc *(Fig. 24a, page 140)*: 169 sc.

Note: Loop a short piece of yarn around any stitch to mark last row as **right** side.

Row 2: Ch 1, turn; sc in first sc, ch 1, skip next sc, sc in next 5 sc, (ch 3, skip next 3 sc, sc in next 5 sc) across to last 2 sc, ch 1, skip next sc, sc in last sc changing to Ecru: 107 sc.

Row 3: Ch 1, turn; sc in first sc, working in **front** of next ch-1, dc in sc one row **below** ch-1, ch 1, (skip next sc, sc in next sc, ch 1) twice, ★ skip next sc, working in **front** of next ch-3, dc in **next** 3 sc one row **below** ch-3, ch 1, (skip next sc, sc in next sc, ch 1) twice; repeat from ★ across to last 3 sts, skip next sc, working in **front** of next ch-1, dc in sc one row **below** ch-1, sc in last sc changing to Green.

Row 4: Ch 1, turn; sc in first 2 sts, working **behind** next ch-1, dc in sc one row **below** ch-1, (ch 1, skip next sc, working **behind** next ch-1, dc in sc one row **below** ch-1) twice, ★ sc in next dc, ch 1, skip next dc, sc in next dc, working **behind** next ch-1, dc in sc one row **below** ch-1, (ch 1, skip next sc, working **behind** next ch-1, dc in sc one row **below** ch-1) twice; repeat from ★ across to last 2 sts, sc in last 2 sts changing to Ecru in last sc.

Row 5: Ch 1, turn; sc in first 3 sts, working in **front** of next ch-1, dc in sc one row **below** ch-1, ch 1, skip next dc, working in **front** of next ch-1, dc in sc one row **below** ch-1, ★ (sc in next 2 sts, working in **front** of next ch-1, dc in st one row **below** ch-1) twice, ch 1, skip next dc, working in **front** of next ch-1, dc in sc one row **below** ch-1; repeat from ★ across to last 3 sts, sc in last 3 sts changing to Green in last sc.

Row 6: Ch 1, turn; sc in first sc, ★ ch 3, skip next 3 sts, working **behind** next ch-1, dc in dc one row **below** ch-1, ch 3, skip next 3 sts, sc in next st; repeat from ★ across changing to Ecru in last sc.

Row 7: Ch 1, turn; sc in first sc, ★ working in **front** of next ch-3, dc in **next** 3 sts one row **below** ch-3, ch 1, skip next dc, working in **front** of next ch-3, dc in **next** 3 sts one row **below** ch-3, sc in next sc; repeat from ★ across changing to Pink in last sc.

Row 8: Ch 1, turn; sc in first sc, ch 2, skip next 2 dc, sc in next dc, working **behind** next ch-1, dc in dc one row **below** ch-1, sc in next dc, ★ (ch 2, skip next 2 dc, sc in next st) twice, working **behind** next ch-1, dc in dc one row **below** ch-1, sc in next dc; repeat from ★ across to last 3 sts, ch 2, skip next 2 dc, sc in last sc changing to Ecru.

Row 9: Ch 1, turn; sc in first sc, ★ working in **front** of next ch-2, dc in **next** 2 dc one row **below** ch-2, ch 3, skip next 3 sts, working in **front** of next ch-2, dc in **next** 2 dc one row **below** ch-2, sc in next sc; repeat from ★ across changing to Pink in last sc.

Row 10: Ch 1, turn; sc in first sc, ch 1, skip next dc, sc in next dc, working **behind** next ch-3, dc in **next** 3 sts one row **below** ch-3, sc in next dc, ★ ch 3, skip next 3 sts, sc in next dc, working **behind** next ch-3, dc in **next** 3 sts one row **below** ch-3, sc in next dc; repeat from ★ across to last 2 sts, ch 1, skip next dc, sc in last sc changing to Ecru.

Row 11: Ch 1, turn; sc in first sc, working in **front** of next ch-1, dc in dc one row **below** ch-1, sc in next 5 sts, ★ working in **front** of next ch-3, dc in **next** 3 sts one row **below** ch-3, sc in next 5 sts; repeat from ★ across to last 2 sts, working in **front** of next ch-1, dc in dc one row **below** ch-1, sc in last sc.

Row 12: Ch 1, turn; sc in first sc, (ch 1, skip next st, sc in next st) across changing to Green in last sc.

Continued on page 38.

FIELD OF DAFFODILS

A field of dimensional daffodils blooms on this lovely afghan! Easy to make with double crochets and chain spaces, the flowers are worked separately and attached to the centers of the hexagons. A helpful placement chart guides the assembly of the motifs, which are whipstitched together.

Finished Size: 51" x 68"

MATERIALS

Worsted Weight Yarn:
- Green - 25 ounces, (710 grams, 1,100 yards)
- Lt Yellow - 22 ounces, (620 grams, 970 yards)
- Yellow - 19 ounces, (540 grams, 840 yards)
- Lt Green - 18 ounces, (510 grams, 795 yards)
- White - 13 ounces, (370 grams, 575 yards)

Crochet hooks, sizes H (5.00 mm) **and** I (5.50 mm) **or** sizes needed for gauge

Yarn needle

GAUGE: Each Motif = 6¹/₂"
(from straight edge to straight edge)

MOTIF (Make 83)

With Yellow and larger size hook, ch 5; join with slip st to form a ring.

Rnd 1 (Right side)**:** Ch 3 **(counts as first dc, now and throughout)**, dc in ring, (ch 1, 2 dc in ring) 5 times, sc in first dc to form last sp: 12 dc.

Note: Loop a short piece of yarn around any stitch to mark last round as **right** side.

Rnd 2: Ch 3, (dc, ch 1, 2 dc) in same sp, ch 1, ★ (2 dc, ch 1, 2 dc) in next ch-1 sp, ch 1; repeat from ★ around; join with slip st to first dc, finish off: 24 dc.

Rnd 3: With **right** side facing, join Lt Yellow with slip st in first ch-1 sp; ch 3, (dc, ch 1, 2 dc) in same sp (corner made), ch 1, 2 dc in next ch-1 sp, ch 1, ★ (2 dc, ch 1, 2 dc) in next ch-1 sp, ch 1, 2 dc in next ch-1 sp, ch 1; repeat from ★ around; join with slip st to first dc, finish off: 36 dc.

Rnd 4: With **right** side facing, join White with slip st in first corner ch-1 sp; ch 3, (dc, ch 1, 2 dc) in same sp, ch 1, (2 dc in next ch-1 sp, ch 1) twice, ★ (2 dc, ch 1, 2 dc) in next corner ch-1 sp, ch 1, (2 dc in next ch-1 sp, ch 1) twice; repeat from ★ around; join with slip st to first dc, finish off: 48 dc.

Rnd 5: With **right** side facing, join Lt Green with slip st in first corner ch-1 sp; ch 3, (dc, ch 1, 2 dc) in same sp, ch 1, (2 dc in next ch-1 sp, ch 1) 3 times, ★ (2 dc, ch 1, 2 dc) in next corner ch-1 sp, ch 1, (2 dc in next ch-1 sp, ch 1) 3 times; repeat from ★ around; join with slip st to first dc, finish off: 60 dc.

Rnd 6: With **right** side facing, join Green with slip st in first corner ch-1 sp; ch 3, (dc, ch 1, 2 dc) in same sp, ch 1, (2 dc in next ch-1 sp, ch 1) 4 times, ★ (2 dc, ch 1, 2 dc) in next corner ch-1 sp, ch 1, (2 dc in next ch-1 sp, ch 1) 4 times; repeat from ★ around; join with slip st to first dc, finish off: 72 dc.

HALF MOTIF (Make 10)

With Yellow and larger size hook, ch 5; join with slip st to form a ring.

Row 1 (Right side)**:** Ch 4 **(counts as first dc plus ch 1, now and throughout)**, (2 dc in ring, ch 1) 3 times, dc in ring; finish off: 8 dc.

Note: Mark last row as **right** side.

Row 2: With **right** side facing, join Yellow with slip st in first ch-1 sp; ch 4, dc in same sp, ch 1, ★ (2 dc, ch 1, 2 dc) in next ch-1 sp (corner made), ch 1; repeat from ★ once **more**, (dc, ch 1, dc) in last ch-1 sp; finish off: 12 dc.

Row 3: With **right** side facing, join Lt Yellow with slip st in first ch-1 sp; ch 4, dc in same sp, ch 1, 2 dc in next ch-1 sp, ch 1, ★ (2 dc, ch 1, 2 dc) in next corner ch-1 sp, ch 1, 2 dc in next ch-1 sp, ch 1; repeat from ★ once **more**, (dc, ch 1, dc) in last ch-1 sp; finish off: 18 dc.

Row 4: With **right** side facing, join White with slip st in first ch-1 sp; ch 4, dc in same sp, ch 1, (2 dc in next ch-1 sp, ch 1) twice, ★ (2 dc, ch 1, 2 dc) in next corner ch-1 sp, ch 1, (2 dc in next ch-1 sp, ch 1) twice; repeat from ★ once **more**, (dc, ch 1, dc) in last ch-1 sp; finish off: 24 dc.

Row 5: With **right** side facing, join Lt Green with slip st in first ch-1 sp; ch 4, dc in same sp, ch 1, (2 dc in next ch-1 sp, ch 1) 3 times, ★ (2 dc, ch 1, 2 dc) in next corner ch-1 sp, ch 1, (2 dc in next ch-1 sp, ch 1) 3 times; repeat from ★ once **more**, (dc, ch 1, dc) in last ch-1 sp; finish off: 30 dc.

Row 6: With **right** side facing, join Green with slip st in first ch-1 sp; ch 4, dc in same sp, ch 1, (2 dc in next ch-1 sp, ch 1) 4 times, ★ (2 dc, ch 1, 2 dc) in next corner ch-1 sp, ch 1, (2 dc in next ch-1 sp, ch 1) 4 times; repeat from ★ once **more**, (dc, ch 1, dc) in last ch-1 sp; finish off: 36 dc.

Continued on page 39.

ST. PATRICK'S WRAP

*Bring the luck o' the Irish to your decor with this charming green
and ecru afghan. Mile-a-minute strips of shells and treble crochet
cables accent the motifs, which feature airy four-leaf designs.*

Finished Size: 49" x 70"

MATERIALS
Worsted Weight Yarn:
Ecru - 25 ounces, (710 grams, 1,645 yards)
Green - 16 ounces, (450 grams, 1,055 yards)
Crochet hook, size J (6.00 mm) **or** size needed
for gauge

GAUGE: Each Square (Strip A) = 4¹/₂"

STITCH GUIDE

DC DECREASE (uses next 2 sts)
★ YO, insert hook in **next** st, YO and pull up a loop, YO
and draw through 2 loops on hook; repeat from ★ once
more, YO and draw through all 3 loops on hook **(counts
as one dc)**.

SC DECREASE (uses next 2 sts)
Pull up a loop in next 2 sts, YO and draw through all 3
loops on hook **(counts as one sc)**.

POPCORN
4 Dc in st or sp indicated, drop loop from hook, insert
hook in first dc of 4-dc group, hook dropped loop and
draw through *(Fig. 10a, page 137)*.

BEGINNING POPCORN
Ch 3, 3 dc in st or sp indicated, drop loop from hook,
insert hook in top of beginning ch, hook dropped loop and
draw through.

STRIP A

SQUARE (Make 28)
With Green, ch 4; join with slip st to form a ring.
Rnd 1 (Right side)**:** Ch 6 **(counts as first dc plus ch 3, now
and throughout)**, (3 dc in ring, ch 3) 3 times, 2 dc in ring;
join with slip st to first dc: 12 dc.
Note: Loop a short piece of yarn around any stitch to mark last
round as **right** side.
Rnd 2: Slip st in first ch-3 sp, ch 3 **(counts as first dc, now
and throughout)**, (2 dc, ch 3, 3 dc) in same sp, dc in next
3 dc, ★ (3 dc, ch 3, 3 dc) in next ch-3 sp (corner), dc in next
3 dc; repeat from ★ around; join with slip st to first dc,
finish off: 36 dc.

Rnd 3: With **right** side facing, join Ecru with slip st in any
corner ch-3 sp; ch 3, (dc, ch 3, 2 dc) in same sp, dc in next
9 dc, ★ (2 dc, ch 3, 2 dc) in next ch-3 sp, dc in next 9 dc;
repeat from ★ around; join with slip st to first dc, finish off.

END TRIANGLE (Make 4)
With Green, ch 4; join with slip st to form a ring.
Row 1 (Right side)**:** Ch 3, (2 dc, ch 3, 3 dc) in ring: 6 dc.
Note: Mark last row as **right** side.
Row 2: Ch 3, turn; dc in same st and in next 2 dc, (3 dc, ch 3,
3 dc) in next ch-3 sp, dc in next 2 dc, 2 dc in last dc; finish off:
14 dc.
Edging: With **right** side facing, join Ecru with slip st in ch-3 sp;
ch 3, (dc, ch 3, 2 dc) in same sp, dc in next 6 dc, 5 dc in last dc
(corner), place marker around center dc for joining placement,
2 dc in end of each of next 2 rows, 3 dc in beginning ring, 2 dc
in end of each of next 2 rows; working across Row 2, 5 dc in
first dc (corner), place marker around center dc for joining
placement, dc in next dc and in each dc around; join with slip st
to first dc, finish off.

JOINING

Strips are assembled by joining 14 Squares into 2 vertical Strips,
then by joining End Triangles to ends of each Strip; do **not** join
Strips.
Join as follows:
With **wrong** sides together and working through inside loops
only of **each** stitch on **both** pieces, join Ecru with slip st in
center ch of any corner; ch 1, sc in same st and in each st
across to center ch of next corner, sc in center ch; finish off.
Mark one End Triangle as bottom.

Continued on page 36.

STRIP B
SQUARE (Make 9)

Rnds 1-3: Work same as Strip A.

Rnd 4: With **right** side facing, join Green with slip st in any corner ch-3 sp; ch 3, (2 dc, ch 3, 3 dc) in same sp, dc in next 2 dc, work Popcorn in next dc, (dc in next 3 dc, work Popcorn in next dc) twice, dc in next 2 dc, ★ (3 dc, ch 3, 3 dc) in next ch-3 sp, dc in next 2 dc, work Popcorn in next dc, (dc in next 3 dc, work Popcorn in next dc) twice, dc in next 2 dc; repeat from ★ around; join with slip st to first dc, finish off: 12 Popcorns.

Rnd 5: With **right** side facing, join Ecru with slip st in any corner ch-3 sp; work (beginning Popcorn, ch 3, Popcorn) in same sp, dc in next 19 sts, ★ work (Popcorn, ch 3, Popcorn) in next ch-3 sp, dc in next 19 sts; repeat from ★ around; join with slip st to beginning Popcorn, finish off: 8 Popcorns.

Join Squares in same manner as before to form a Strip.

END CAP

Row 1: With **right** side of Strip facing, join Green with slip st in center ch of right corner ch-3 sp on end Square; ch 3, dc decrease, dc in next 19 dc, dc decrease, dc in next ch: 23 dc.

Row 2: Ch 1, turn; sc decrease, sc in next 19 dc, sc decrease: 21 sc.

Row 3: Ch 3, turn; dc decrease, dc in next 15 sc, dc decrease, dc in last sc: 19 dc.

Row 4: Ch 1, turn; sc decrease, sc in next 15 dc, sc decrease: 17 sc.

Row 5: Ch 1, turn; sc decrease, sc in next 3 sc, hdc in next 3 sc, dc in next sc, hdc in next 3 sc, sc in next 3 sc, sc decrease; finish off: 15 sts.

END CAP TRIM

With **right** side facing, join Ecru with slip st in same st as first dc on Row 1 of End Cap; working in end of rows, dc in first row, place marker around dc just made for joining placement, dc in same row and in next row, 2 dc in next row, dc in next row, skip last row; working across Row 5, 3 dc in first sc, 2 dc in next sc, dc in next 5 sts, (dc, ch 2, dc) in next dc, dc in next 5 sts, 2 dc in next sc, 3 dc in last sc; working in end of rows, skip first row, (dc in next row, 2 dc in next row) twice, place marker around dc just made for joining placement, slip st in same st as last dc on Row 1 of End Cap; finish off.

Repeat for second End Cap.

Mark one End Cap as bottom.

STRIP C (Make 6)

With Green, ch 6; join with slip st to form a ring.

Row 1 (Right side): Ch 3, (2 dc, ch 2, 3 dc) in ring.

Note: Mark last row as **right** side and bottom edge.

Rows 2-78: Ch 3, turn; (3 dc, ch 2, 3 dc) in ch-2 sp, skip next 2 dc, dc in last dc.

Finish off.

EDGING

With **right** side facing, join Ecru with slip st in beginning ring; ch 4 **(counts as first tr)**, (5 tr, ch 1, 6 tr) in same sp, place markers around first and last tr made for joining placement, skip first row, 3 dc in end of each row across, (6 tr, ch 1, 6 tr) in next ch-2 sp, place markers around first and last tr just made for joining placement, 3 dc in end of each row across to last row, skip last row; join with slip st to first tr, finish off: 77 3-dc groups **each** side.

STRIP D (Make 2)

With Ecru, ch 15 **loosely**, slip st in tenth ch from hook **(first loop made)**, ch 7 **loosely**.

Row 1 (Right side): Dc in fourth ch from hook **(3 skipped chs count as first dc)** and in next 3 chs, ch 10, skip first loop, dc in last 5 chs: 10 dc.

Note #1: Mark last row as **right** side and bottom edge.

Note #2: When working remaining rows, hold ch-10 loops on **right** side of work.

Rows 2-99: Ch 3, turn; dc in next 4 dc, ch 10, dc in last 5 dc: 10 dc.

Row 100: Ch 3, turn; dc in next 4 dc, ch 2, dc in last 5 dc; do **not** finish off.

BRAIDING

Beginning on Row 1 and working from bottom to top, insert hook from **front** to **back** into first ch-10 loop, ★ pull next ch-10 loop through loop on hook; repeat from ★ to top of Strip, leaving last loop free for Edging.

ST. PATRICK'S WRAP

EDGING

Ch 3, place marker around dc just made for joining placement, turn; (dc, sc) in same st, hdc in next 2 dc, skip next 2 dc; working **over** ch-10 loop, (4 tr, ch 2, 4 tr) in next ch-2 sp, skip next 2 dc, hdc in next 2 dc, (sc, 2 dc) in last dc, place marker around last dc made for joining placement; working in end of rows, 2 dc in each of first 7 rows, (3 dc in next row, 2 dc in each of next 2 rows) across; working in free loops of beginning ch *(Fig. 23b, page 140)*, dc in first ch, place marker around last dc made for joining placement, (dc, sc) in same st, hdc in next 2 chs, skip next 2 chs, (4 tr, ch 2, 4 tr) in next sp (base of ch-10 loop), skip next 2 chs, hdc in next 2 chs, (sc, 2 dc) in next ch, place marker around last dc made for joining placement; working in end of rows, 2 dc in each of first 7 rows, (3 dc in next row, 2 dc in each of next 2 rows) across; join with slip st to first dc, finish off: 231 dc **each** side **between** markers.

ASSEMBLY

Note: Because of differences in stitch counts, it will be necessary to work into some stitches twice or to sometimes skip a stitch. Pin the edges of the Strips together evenly before joining.
Lay Strips out in the following order, with all markers at bottom: C - A - C - D - C - B - C - D - C - A - C.
Beginning and ending in marked sts, join all Strips in same manner as before.

BORDER

With **right** side facing, join Ecru with slip st in any st; ch 1, sc evenly around, increasing and decreasing as necessary to keep Afghan lying flat; join with slip st to first sc, finish off.

COUNTRY PLAID Continued from page 26.

PLACEMENT CHART

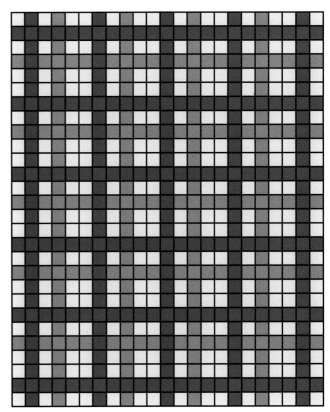

BABY'S RAINBOW GRANNY Continued from page 28.

Rnd 2 (Eyelet rnd): Slip st in first ch-3 sp, ch 3, (dc, ch 3, 2 dc) in same sp, ★ † ch 1, skip next sc, (dc in next sc, ch 1) across to within 1 sc of next ch-3 sp, skip next sc †, (2 dc, ch 3, 2 dc) in next ch-3 sp; repeat from ★ 2 times **more**, then repeat from † to † once; join with slip st to first dc.

Rnd 3: Ch 5, dc in same st, ch 2, skip next dc, (dc, ch 2) 4 times in next ch-3 sp, ★ skip next dc, (dc, ch 2) twice in next dc, [dc in next dc, ch 2, (dc, ch 2) twice in next dc] across to within 1 dc of next ch-3 sp, skip next dc, (dc, ch 2) 4 times in next ch-3 sp; repeat from ★ 2 times **more**, skip next dc, [(dc, ch 2) twice in next dc, dc in next dc, ch 2] across; join with slip st to third ch of beginning ch-5, finish off.

Rnd 4: With **right** side facing, join Pink with sc in any dc; ch 2, (sc in next dc, ch 2) around; join with slip st to first sc, finish off.

Rnd 5: With **right** side facing, join Green with sc in any sc; ch 2, (sc in next sc, ch 2) around; join with slip st to first sc, finish off.

Rnd 6: With **right** side facing, join Yellow with sc in any sc; ch 2, (sc in next sc, ch 2) around; join with slip st to first sc, finish off.

Rnd 7: With **right** side facing, join Blue with sc in any sc; ch 2, (sc in next sc, ch 2) around; join with slip st to first sc, finish off.

Weave ribbon through Eyelet rnd along one side of Afghan, leaving 10" at each end: Repeat for remaining three sides. Tie ends in a bow at each corner.

TULIP KISSES Continued from page 30.

Row 13: Ch 1, turn; sc in first sc, (working **behind** next ch-1, dc in st one row **below** ch-1, sc in next sc) across.

Row 14: Ch 1, turn; sc in first 2 sts, ch 1, (skip next sc, sc in next dc, ch 1) across to last 3 sts, skip next sc, sc in last 2 sts changing to Ecru in last sc.

Row 15: Ch 1, turn; sc in first 2 sc, working in **front** of next ch-1, dc in sc one row **below** ch-1, ★ sc in next sc, working **behind** next ch-1, dc in sc one row **below** ch-1, sc in next sc, working in **front** of next ch-1, dc in sc one row **below** ch-1; repeat from ★ across to last 2 sc, sc in last 2 sc.

Row 16: Ch 1, turn; sc in first sc, (ch 1, skip next sc, sc in next st) across; finish off.

SECOND SIDE

Row 1: With **wrong** side facing and working in free loops of beginning ch *(Fig. 23b, page 140)*, join Ecru with sc in ch at base of first sc *(see Joining With Sc, page 140)*; (ch 1, skip next ch, sc in next ch) across changing to Pink in last sc: 85 sc.

Row 2: Ch 1, turn; sc in first sc, (working **behind** next ch-1, dc in ch one row **below** ch-1, sc in next sc) across.

Row 3: Ch 1, turn; sc in first 2 sts, ch 1, (skip next dc, sc in next dc, ch 1) across to last 3 sts, skip next sc, sc in last 2 sts changing to Ecru in last sc.

Row 4: Ch 1, turn; sc in first 2 sc, working in **front** of next ch-1, dc in sc one row **below** ch-1, ★ sc in next sc, working **behind** next ch-1, dc in sc one row **below** ch-1, sc in next sc, working in **front** of next ch-1, dc in sc one row **below** ch-1; repeat from ★ across to last 2 sc, sc in last 2 sc.

Row 5: Ch 1, turn; sc in first sc, (ch 1, skip next sc, sc in next st) across; finish off.

ASSEMBLY

Using Ecru, whipstitch Strips together *(Fig. 28a, page 142)* beginning in first corner sc and ending in next corner sc.

EDGING

TOP

With **right** side facing and working across last row, join Ecru with slip st in first sc; slip st in next ch-1 sp, (ch 1, skip next sc, slip st in next ch-1 sp) across to last sc, slip st in last sc; finish off.

BOTTOM

With **right** side facing and working across last row, join Ecru with slip st in first sc; slip st in next ch-1 sp, (ch 1, skip next sc, slip st in next ch-1 sp) across to last sc, slip st in last sc; finish off.

Holding three strands of Ecru together, add fringe in each ch-1 sp across short edges of Afghan *(Figs. 29a & c, page 142)*.

DAFFODIL (Make 83)
TRUMPET
With Yellow and smaller size hook, ch 4; join with slip st to form a ring.

Rnd 1 (Wrong side): 12 Sc in ring; do **not** join, place marker.

Note: Do not join at end of rounds. Place a 2" scrap piece of yarn before the first stitch of each round, moving marker after each round is complete.

Rnd 2: Sc in Front Loop Only of each sc around *(Fig. 22, page 140)*.

Rnds 3-5: Sc in both loops of each sc around.

Rnd 6: Sc in each sc around; slip st in next sc, finish off.

PETALS
Note: To work **double treble crochet (abbreviated dtr)**, YO 3 times, insert hook in st indicated, YO and pull up a loop, (YO and draw through 2 loops on hook) 4 times *(Figs. 8a & b, page 136)*.

With Trumpet opening toward you and working in free loops on Rnd 1 *(Fig. 23a, page 140)*, join Lt Yellow with slip st in any sc; ch 1, in same st work (sc, 2 dc, tr, dtr, tr, 2 dc, sc), skip next sc, ★ in next sc work (sc, 2 dc, tr, dtr, tr, 2 dc, sc), skip next sc; repeat from ★ around; join with slip st to first sc, finish off leaving a long end for sewing: 6 Petals.

ASSEMBLY
With Green and using Placement Diagram as a guide, whipstitch Motifs together forming 11 horizontal strips *(Fig. 28a, page 142)*, beginning in first corner ch-1 and ending in next corner ch-1; then whipstitch strips together in same manner.

EDGING
With **right** side facing, join Green with slip st in top right corner ch-1 sp (point A); ch 3, (dc, ch 1, 2 dc) in same sp, † ch 1, (2 dc in next ch-1 sp, ch 1) 5 times, (2 dc, ch 1, 2 dc) in next corner ch-1 sp, ch 1, ★ (2 dc in next ch-1 sp, ch 1) 4 times, dc in next ch-1 sp, skip next joining, dc in next ch-1 sp on next Motif, ch 1, (2 dc in next ch-1 sp, ch 1) 4 times, (2 dc, ch 1, 2 dc) in next corner ch-1 sp, ch 1; repeat from ★ 6 times **more**, (2 dc in next ch-1 sp, ch 1) 5 times, (2 dc, ch 1, 2 dc) in next corner ch-1 sp, ch 1, (2 dc in next ch-1 sp, ch 1) 6 times, skip next joining, (2 dc in end of next row, ch 1) 6 times, 2 dc in beginning ring, ch 1, (2 dc in end of next row, ch 1) 6 times, [(2 dc in next ch-1 sp, ch 1) 7 times, (2 dc in end of next row, ch 1) 6 times, 2 dc in beginning ring, ch 1, (2 dc in end of next row, ch 1) 6 times] 4 times, (2 dc in next ch-1 sp, ch 1) 6 times †, (2 dc, ch 1, 2 dc) in next corner ch-1 sp, repeat from † to † once; join with slip st to first dc, finish off.

Sew a Daffodil to center of each Motif.

PLACEMENT DIAGRAM

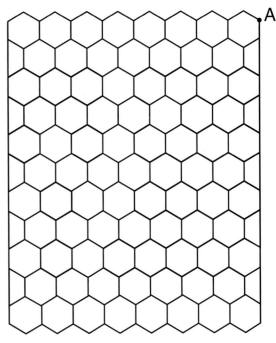

COMING UP ROSES

A rosy accent for the bedroom, this afghan gets its elegant texture from front and back post double crochets and puffy cluster stitches. The wrap is richly finished with a feminine fringe.

STITCH GUIDE

FRONT POST DOUBLE CROCHET (abbreviated FPdc)
YO, insert hook from **front** to **back** around post of next dc, YO and pull up a loop *(Fig. 13, page 137)*, (YO and draw through 2 loops on hook) twice.

BACK POST DOUBLE CROCHET (abbreviated BPdc)
YO, insert hook from **back** to **front** around post of next dc, YO and pull up a loop *(Fig. 14, page 138)*, (YO and draw through 2 loops on hook) twice.

CLUSTER
YO, insert hook in st or sp indicated, YO and pull up a loop, YO and draw through 2 loops on hook, ★ YO, insert hook in **same** st or sp, YO and pull up a loop, YO and draw through 2 loops on hook; repeat from ★ 3 times **more**, YO and draw through all 6 loops on hook *(Figs. 9a & b, page 137)*. Push Cluster to **right** side.

DECREASE (uses next 3 sts)
★ YO, insert hook in **next** st, YO and pull up a loop, YO and draw through 2 loops on hook; repeat from ★ 2 times **more**, YO and draw through all 4 loops on hook.

Note: Each row is worked across length of Afghan.

Ch 222 **loosely**.

Row 1 (Right side): Dc in fourth ch from hook **(3 skipped chs count as first dc)** and in each ch across: 220 dc.

Note: Loop a short piece of yarn around any stitch to mark last row as **right** side.

Rows 2 and 3: Ch 3 **(counts as first dc, now and throughout)**, turn; dc in next dc and in each dc across.

Row 4: Ch 3, turn; (work BPdc around next dc, work FPdc around next dc) across to last dc, dc in last dc.

Rows 5 and 6: Ch 3, turn; dc in next st and in each st across.

Row 7: Ch 3, turn; skip next 2 dc, (3 dc in next dc, skip next 2 dc) across to last dc, dc in last dc: 72 3-dc groups.

Row 8: Ch 1, turn; sc in first 2 dc, (work Cluster in next dc, sc in next 2 dc) across: 72 Clusters.

Row 9: Ch 3, turn; dc in next sc, (ch 1, dc in next 2 sc) across.

Row 10: Ch 1, turn; sc in first 2 dc, (work Cluster in next ch-1 sp, sc in next 2 dc) across.

Continued on page 51.

Finished Size: 46¹/₂" x 67¹/₂"

MATERIALS
Worsted Weight Yarn:
49 ounces,
(1,390 grams, 3,360 yards)
Crochet hook, size I (5.50 mm) **or** size
needed for gauge

GAUGE: 18 dc and 12 rows (1 repeat) = 5¹/₂"

SPRING DREAM

The delicate hues of spring flowers inspired this dreamy afghan. Each motif is created with textured rows of simple stitches and bordered with double crochets and chain spaces. Joining the squares with the rows going in alternating directions produces the subtle checkerboard effect.

Finished Size: 47¹/₂" x 67"

MATERIALS

Worsted Weight Yarn:
    46 ounces, (1,310 grams, 3,155 yards)
Crochet hook, size H (5.00 mm) **or** size needed
    for gauge
Yarn needle

GAUGE: Each Square = 6¹/₂"

SQUARE (Make 70)

Ch 13 **loosely**.

Row 1 (Right side)**:** Sc in second ch from hook and in each ch across: 12 sc.

Note: Loop a short piece of yarn around any stitch to mark last row as **right** side.

Rows 2-15: Ch 1, turn; sc in first st, ★ insert hook in **same** st, YO and pull up a loop, insert hook in **next** st, YO and pull up a loop, YO and draw through all 3 loops on hook; repeat from ★ across: 12 sts.

Do **not** finish off.

BORDER

Rnd 1: Ch 3 **(counts as first dc, now and throughout)**, working in end of rows, (dc, ch 1, 2 dc) in last row, work 12 dc evenly spaced across to first row, (2 dc, ch 1, 2 dc) in first row; working in free loops of beginning ch **(Fig. 23b, page 140)**, dc in first 12 chs; working in end of rows, (2 dc, ch 1, 2 dc) in first row, work 12 dc evenly spaced across to last row, (2 dc, ch 1, 2 dc) in last row; dc in each st across; join with slip st to first dc: 64 dc.

Rnd 2: Ch 3, dc in next dc, ★ (2 dc, ch 1, 2 dc) in next ch-1 sp, dc in each dc across to next corner; repeat from ★ around; join with slip st to first dc, finish off: 80 dc.

ASSEMBLY

Whipstitch Squares together, forming 7 vertical strips of 10 Squares each **(Fig. 28b, page 142)**, alternating the direction of each Square, and beginning in ch of first corner and ending in ch of next corner; then whipstitch strips together in same manner.

EDGING

Rnd 1: With **right** side facing and working in Back Loops Only **(Fig. 22, page 140)**, join yarn with slip st in any corner ch; ch 3, (dc, ch 1, 2 dc) in same st, dc in each st and in each joining across to next corner ch, ★ (2 dc, ch 1, 2 dc) in corner ch, dc in each st and in each joining across to next corner ch; repeat from ★ around; join with slip st to first dc.

Rnd 2: Ch 3, working in both loops, dc in next dc, ★ (2 dc, ch 1, 2 dc) in corner ch-1 sp, dc in each dc across to next corner ch-1 sp; repeat from ★ around; join with slip st to first dc, finish off.

EASTER EGGS

Offset with rows of white V-stitches, the pastel clusters in this lacy afghan resemble tiny colored eggs — making it a delightful Easter accessory! Rounds of V-stitches and yellow "eggs" form the edging.

Finished Size: 47" x 63"

MATERIALS
    Worsted Weight Yarn:
        White - 18 ounces, (510 grams, 1,185 yards)
        Yellow - 9 ounces, (260 grams, 595 yards)
        Aqua - 6 ounces, (170 grams, 395 yards)
        Pink - 3 ounces, (90 grams, 200 yards)
    Crochet hook, size K (6.50 mm) **or** size needed
        for gauge

GAUGE: 19 sts = 5¼" and 8 rows = 4"

COLOR SEQUENCE
3 Rows White *(Fig. 24a, page 140)*, 2 rows Aqua, 3 rows White, 2 rows Yellow, 3 rows White, † 2 rows Pink, 3 rows White, 2 rows Aqua, 3 rows White, 2 rows Yellow, 3 rows White †, repeat from † to † once **more**, 2 rows Aqua, 3 rows White, ★ 2 rows Pink, 3 rows White, 2 rows Yellow, 3 rows White, 2 rows Aqua, 3 rows White; repeat from ★ once **more**.

Note: Each row is worked across length of Afghan.

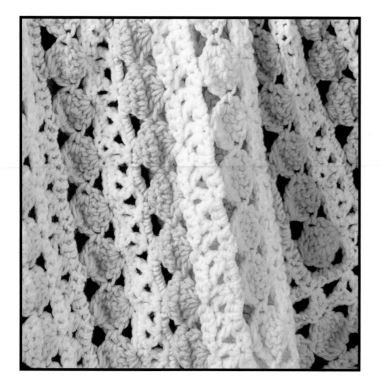

With White, ch 200 **loosely**.

Row 1: Sc in second ch from hook and in each ch across: 199 sc.

*Note: To work **V-St**, (dc, ch 1, dc) in next sc.*

Row 2 (Right side): Ch 3 **(counts as first dc, now and throughout)**, turn; (skip next 2 sc, work V-St) across to last 3 sc, skip next 2 sc, dc in last sc: 65 V-Sts.

*Note: Loop a short piece of yarn around any stitch to mark last row as **right** side.*

Row 3: Ch 1, turn; sc in each dc and in each ch-1 sp across: 197 sc.

Row 4: Ch 3, turn; skip next 2 sc, 5 dc in next sc, (skip next 4 sc, 5 dc in next sc) across to last 3 sc, skip next 2 sc, dc in last sc: 197 dc.

*Note: To work **Cluster** (uses next 5 dc), ★ YO, insert hook in **next** dc, YO and pull up a loop, YO and draw through 2 loops on hook; repeat from ★ 4 times **more**, YO and draw through all 6 loops on hook (Figs. 9c & d, page 137).*

Row 5: Ch 5 **(counts as first dc plus ch 2, now and throughout)**, turn; work Cluster, (ch 4, work Cluster) across to last dc, ch 2, dc in last dc: 39 Clusters.

Row 6: Ch 1, turn; sc in first dc, 3 sc in next ch-2 sp, sc in next Cluster, (4 sc in next ch-4 sp, sc in next Cluster) across to last ch-2 sp, 3 sc in ch-2 sp, sc in last dc: 199 sc.

Row 7: Ch 3, turn; (skip next 2 sc, work V-St) across to last 3 sc, skip next 2 sc, dc in last sc: 65 V-Sts.

Row 8: Ch 1, turn; sc in each dc and in each ch-1 sp across: 197 sc.

Rows 9-78: Repeat Rows 4-8, 14 times.
Do **not** finish off.

Continued on page 51.

ORCHID WHIMSY

Orchid-inspired motifs create a garden of soft comfort on this springtime throw. Each dainty square combines stitches ranging from slip stitches to front post treble crochets. Long, generous fringe enhances the whimsical design.

Finished Size: 46" x 63"

MATERIALS

Worsted Weight Yarn:
   Lilac - 25 ounces, (710 grams, 1,645 yards)
   White - 20 ounces, (570 grams, 1,315 yards)
Crochet hook, size H (5.00 mm) **or** size needed
   for gauge
Yarn needle

GAUGE: Each Square = 8¾"

SQUARE (Make 35)

With Lilac, ch 8; join with slip st to form a ring.

Rnd 1 (Right side)**:** Ch 3 **(counts as first dc, now and throughout)**, 4 dc in ring, ch 3, (5 dc in ring, ch 3) 3 times; join with slip st to first dc, finish off: 20 dc.

Note: Loop a short piece of yarn around any stitch to mark last round as **right** side.

Rnd 2: With **right** side facing, join White with slip st in any ch-3 sp; ch 10, slip st in same sp, sc in next 5 dc, ★ (slip st, ch 10, slip st) in next ch-3 sp, sc in next 5 dc; repeat from ★ around; join with slip st to first slip st: 4 loops.

Rnd 3: Slip st in first loop, ch 3, (6 dc, ch 3, 7 dc) in same loop, skip next 2 sc, dc in next sc, skip next 2 sc, ★ (7 dc, ch 3, 7 dc) in next loop, skip next 2 sc, dc in next sc, skip next 2 sc; repeat from ★ around; join with slip st to first dc, finish off: 60 dc.

Note: To work **Front Post treble crochet (abbreviated FPtr)**, YO twice, insert hook from **front** to **back** around post of st indicated, YO and pull up a loop, (YO and draw through 2 loops on hook) 3 times *(Fig. 15, page 138)*. Skip st behind FPtr.

Rnd 4: With **right** side facing, join Lilac with slip st in any ch-3 sp; ch 1, (sc, ch 3, sc) in same sp, ★ † sc in next 3 dc, hdc in next dc, dc in next 2 dc, skip next dc, work FPtr around next dc, skip next dc, dc in next 2 dc, hdc in next dc, sc in next 3 dc †, (sc, ch 3, sc) in next ch-3 sp; repeat from ★ 2 times **more**, then repeat from † to † once; join with slip st to first sc: 4 FPtr.

Rnd 5: Ch 3, (2 dc, ch 3, 2 dc) in next ch-3 sp, dc in next 6 sts, ch 1, skip next dc, work FPtr around next FPtr, ch 1, ★ skip next dc, dc in next 6 sts, (2 dc, ch 3, 2 dc) in next ch-3 sp, dc in next 6 sts, ch 1, skip next dc, work FPtr around next FPtr, ch 1; repeat from ★ around to last 6 sts, skip next dc, dc in last 5 sts; join with slip st to first dc, finish off.

Rnd 6: With **right** side facing, join White with slip st in any ch-3 sp; ch 3, (dc, ch 3, 2 dc) in same sp, ★ † dc in next 7 dc, work FPtr around next dc, (ch 1, skip next ch, work FPtr around next st) twice, dc in next 7 dc †, (2 dc, ch 3, 2 dc) in next ch-3 sp; repeat from ★ 2 times **more**, then repeat from † to † once; join with slip st to first dc: 12 FPtr.

Rnd 7: Ch 3, dc in next dc, ★ † (2 dc, ch 3, 2 dc) in next ch-3 sp, dc in next 7 dc, work FPtr around next dc, ch 1, skip next dc, (work FPtr around next FPtr, ch 1) 3 times, skip next dc, work FPtr around next dc †, dc in next 7 dc; repeat from ★ 2 times **more**, then repeat from † to † once, dc in last 5 dc; join with slip st to first dc, finish off: 20 FPtr.

Rnd 8: With **right** side facing, join Lilac with slip st in any ch-3 sp; ch 3, (dc, ch 3, 2 dc) in same sp, dc in next dc and in each st and each ch-1 sp across to next ch-3 sp, ★ (2 dc, ch 3, 2 dc) in next ch-3 sp, dc in next dc and in each st and each ch-1 sp across to next ch-3 sp; repeat from ★ around; join with slip st to first dc, finish off: 124 dc.

ASSEMBLY

Using Lilac, whipstitch Squares together forming 5 vertical strips of 7 Squares each *(Fig. 28a, page 142)*, beginning in center ch of first corner ch-3 and ending in center ch of next corner ch-3; then whipstitch strips together in same manner.

Continued on page 50.

GRANDMOTHER'S GARDEN

The colorful blossoms on this nostalgic wrap bring to mind the classic Grandmother's Flower Garden quilt pattern. The hexagon-shaped motifs are joined as you go to create the pretty six-sided afghan.

Finished Size: 63" x 73"

MATERIALS
Worsted Weight Yarn:
Ecru - 47 ounces, (1,330 grams, 2,740 yards)
Peach - 5 ounces, (140 grams, 290 yards)
Lt Rose - 5 ounces, (140 grams, 290 yards)
Rose - 5 ounces, (140 grams, 290 yards)
Lt Blue - 5 ounces, (140 grams, 290 yards)
Blue - 4½ ounces, (130 grams, 260 yards)
Green - 4 ounces, (110 grams, 230 yards)
Crochet hook, size H (5.00 mm) **or** size needed for gauge

GAUGE: Each Motif = 2½" (side to side)

Note: Following Placement Diagram, page 50, begin with left Motif of Row 1, and work across joining Motifs. Color shown in each Motif in Placement Diagram indicates color to use for each Motif.

FIRST MOTIF

Note: To work **Cluster**, ★ YO, insert hook in ring, YO and pull up a loop, YO and draw through 2 loops on hook; repeat from ★ once **more**, YO and draw through all 3 loops on hook *(Figs. 9a & b, page 137)*.
With Ecru, ch 4; join with slip st to form a ring.
Rnd 1 (Right side): Ch 2, dc in ring, ch 3, (work Cluster, ch 3) 5 times; join with slip st to first dc: 6 ch-3 sps.
Note: Loop a short piece of yarn around any stitch to mark last round as **right** side.
Rnd 2: Slip st in first ch-3 sp, ch 3 **(counts as first dc, now and throughout)**, (dc, ch 2, 2 dc) in same sp, ch 1, ★ (2 dc, ch 2, 2 dc) in next ch-3 sp, ch 1; repeat from ★ around; join with slip st to first dc, finish off: 12 sps.

ADDITIONAL MOTIFS

Ch 4; join with slip st to form a ring.
Rnd 1: Work same as First Motif.
Rnd 2: Work One, Two, or Three Side Joining *(Fig. 25, page 140)*.

ONE SIDE JOINING
Slip st in first ch-3 sp, ch 3, (dc, ch 2, 2 dc) in same sp, ch 1, ★ (2 dc, ch 2, 2 dc) in next ch-3 sp, ch 1; repeat from ★ 2 times **more**, 2 dc in next ch-3 sp, ch 1, holding Motifs with **wrong** sides together, slip st in corner sp on **adjacent Motif**, ch 1, 2 dc in same ch-3 sp on **new Motif**, ch 1, slip st in next ch-1 sp on **adjacent Motif**, 2 dc in next ch-3 sp on **new Motif**, ch 1, slip st in next corner sp on **adjacent Motif**, ch 1, 2 dc in same ch-3 sp on **new Motif**, ch 1; join with slip st to first dc, finish off.

TWO SIDE JOINING
Slip st in first ch-3 sp, ch 3, (dc, ch 2, 2 dc) in same sp, ch 1, ★ (2 dc, ch 2, 2 dc) in next ch-3 sp, ch 1; repeat from ★ once **more**, 2 dc in next ch-3 sp, ch 1, holding Motifs with **wrong** sides together, slip st in corner sp on **adjacent Motif**, ch 1, 2 dc in same ch-3 sp on **new Motif**, ch 1, slip st in next ch-1 sp on **adjacent Motif**, 2 dc in next ch-3 sp on **new Motif**, ch 1, (slip st in next corner sp on **adjacent Motif**, ch 1) twice, 2 dc in same ch-3 sp on **new Motif**, ch 1, slip st in next ch-1 sp on **adjacent Motif**, 2 dc in next ch-3 sp on **new Motif**, ch 1, slip st in next corner sp on **adjacent Motif**, ch 1, 2 dc in same ch-3 sp on **new Motif**, ch 1; join with slip st to first dc, finish off.

THREE SIDE JOINING
Slip st in first ch-3 sp, ch 3, (dc, ch 2, 2 dc) in same sp, ch 1, (2 dc, ch 2, 2 dc) in next ch-3 sp, ch 1, 2 dc in next ch-3 sp, ch 1, holding Motifs with **wrong** sides together, slip st in corner sp on **adjacent Motif**, ch 1, 2 dc in same ch-3 sp on **new Motif**, ch 1, slip st in next ch-1 sp on **adjacent Motif**, 2 dc in next ch-3 sp on **new Motif**, ch 1, ★ (slip st in next corner sp on **adjacent Motif**, ch 1) twice, 2 dc in same ch-3 sp on **new Motif**, ch 1, slip st in next ch-1 sp on **adjacent Motif**, 2 dc in next ch-3 sp on **new Motif**, ch 1; repeat from ★ once **more**, slip st in next corner sp on **adjacent Motif**, ch 1, 2 dc in same ch-3 sp on **new Motif**, ch 1; join with slip st to first dc, finish off.

Continued on page 50.

GRANDMOTHER'S GARDEN Continued from page 48.

EDGING

Note: To **decrease**, insert hook in next ch, YO and pull up a loop, skip joining, insert hook in next ch, YO and pull up a loop, YO and draw through all 3 loops on hook.

With **right** side facing, join Ecru with slip st in first ch of any ch-2 sp; ch 1, sc in each ch and in each dc around decreasing at each joining; join with slip st to first sc, finish off.

PLACEMENT DIAGRAM

Row 1 ➛

ORCHID WHIMSY Continued from page 46.

EDGING

Note: To **decrease**, YO, insert hook in next sp, YO and pull up a loop, YO and draw through 2 loops on hook, YO, insert hook in joining, YO and pull up a loop, YO and draw through 2 loops on hook, YO, insert hook in next sp, YO and pull up a loop, YO and draw through 2 loops on hook, YO and draw through all 4 loops on hook.

Rnd 1: With **right** side facing, join White with slip st in any corner ch-3 sp; ch 3, (dc, ch 3, 2 dc) in same sp, ★ † dc in next 31 dc, (decrease, dc in next 31 dc) across to next corner ch-3 sp †, (2 dc, ch 3, 2 dc) in ch-3 sp; repeat from ★ 2 times **more**, then repeat from † to † once; join with slip st to first dc.

Rnd 2: Ch 3, dc in next dc, (2 dc, ch 3, 2 dc) in next corner ch-3 sp, ★ dc in next dc and in each dc across to next corner ch-3 sp, (2 dc, ch 3, 2 dc) in corner ch-3 sp; repeat from ★ 2 times **more**, dc in next dc and in each dc across; join with slip st to first dc, finish off.

Holding four, 15" strands of Lilac together, add fringe evenly across short edges of Afghan (*Figs. 29a & c, page 142*).

EASTER EGGS Continued from page 44.

EDGING

Rnd 1: Ch 1, do **not** turn; working in end of rows, work 141 sc evenly spaced across; working in free loops of beginning ch *(Fig. 23b, page 140)*, 3 sc in ch at base of first sc, skip next ch, sc in each ch across to last 2 chs, skip next ch, 3 sc in last ch; working in end of rows, work 141 sc evenly spaced across; working across Row 78, 3 sc in first sc, sc in each sc across to last sc, 3 sc in last sc; join with slip st to first sc: 684 sc.

Rnd 2: Turn; slip st in first 2 sc, ch 3, 4 dc in same st, † ch 1, skip next 2 sc, work V-St, (ch 1, skip next 3 sc, work V-St) 48 times, ch 1, skip next 2 sc, 5 dc in next sc (corner), ch 1, skip next 3 sc, (work V-St, ch 1, skip next 3 sts) 35 times †, 5 dc in next sc (corner), repeat from † to † once; join with slip st to first dc: 168 V-Sts.

Rnd 3: Ch 1, turn; sc in same st, sc in each ch-1 sp and in each dc across to center dc of next corner, ★ 3 sc in center dc, sc in each dc and in each ch-1 sp across to center dc of next corner; repeat from ★ 2 times **more**, sc in center dc, place marker around sc just made for Rnd 4 placement, 2 sc in same st, sc in last dc; join with slip st to first sc, finish off: 704 sc.

Rnd 4: With **wrong** side facing, join Yellow with slip st in marked sc; ch 3, 4 dc in same st, † skip next 5 sc, 5 dc in next sc, (skip next 4 sc, 5 dc in next sc) 38 times, skip next 5 sc, 5 dc in next sc, skip next sc, 5 dc in next sc, skip next 5 sc, 5 dc in next sc, (skip next 4 sc, 5 dc in next sc) 28 times, skip next sc †, 5 dc in next sc, repeat from † to † once; join with slip st to first dc: 710 dc.

Rnd 5: Turn; slip st in next dc, ch 2, (YO, insert hook in **next** dc, YO and pull up a loop, YO and draw through 2 loops on hook) 4 times, YO and draw through all 5 loops on hook, † (ch 4, work Cluster) 29 times, ch 7, work Cluster, (ch 4, work Cluster) 40 times, ch 7 †, work Cluster, repeat from † to † once; join with slip st to first st, finish off: 142 ch-sps.

Rnd 6: With **wrong** side facing, join White with slip st in same st as joining; ch 1, sc in same st, 9 sc in next ch-7 sp, sc in next Cluster, ★ (4 sc in next ch-4 sp, sc in next Cluster) across to next ch-7 sp, 9 sc in ch-7 sp, sc in next Cluster; repeat from ★ 2 times **more**, 4 sc in next ch-4 sp, (sc in next Cluster, 4 sc in next ch-4 sp) across; join with slip st to first sc: 730 sc.

Rnd 7: Slip st in next 5 sc, ch 3, turn; 4 dc in same st, † ch 1, skip next 5 sts, work V-St, ch 1, (skip next 3 sc, work V-St, ch 1) 36 times, skip next 4 sc, 5 dc in next sc, ch 1, skip next 4 sc, work V-St, ch 1, (skip next 3 sc, work V-St, ch 1) 50 times, skip next 4 sc †, 5 dc in next sc, repeat from † to † once; join with slip st to first dc: 176 V-Sts.

Rnds 8 and 9: Ch 1, turn; sc evenly around, working 3 sc in each corner; join with slip st to first sc.
Finish off.

COMING UP ROSES Continued from page 40.

Row 11: Ch 5 **(counts as first dc plus ch 2)**, turn; (decrease, ch 2) across to last sc, dc in last sc.
Row 12: Ch 1, turn; sc in each ch and in each st across: 220 sc.
Rows 13-15: Ch 3, turn; dc in next st and in each st across.
Repeat Rows 4-15 until Afghan measures 46¹/₂", ending by working Row 6.
Finish off.

Holding four strands of yarn together, add fringe evenly across short edges of Afghan *(Figs. 29b & d, page 142)*.

BABY'S KEEPSAKE

*A light coverlet for pleasant spring mornings, this
delicate baby afghan features a latticework of very simple
stitches. Gentle scallops finish the openwork edging.*

CENTER

Ch 118 **loosely**.

Row 1 (Right side): Sc in second ch from hook, (ch 5, skip next 3 chs, sc in next ch) twice, ch 1, skip next ch, 3 dc in next ch, ch 1, skip next ch, sc in next ch, ★ (ch 5, skip next 3 chs, sc in next ch) 3 times, ch 1, skip next ch, 3 dc in next ch, ch 1, skip next ch, sc in next ch; repeat from ★ across to last 8 chs, (ch 5, skip next 3 chs, sc in next ch) twice: 21 dc.

Note: Loop a short piece of yarn around any stitch to mark last row as **right** side.

Row 2: Ch 5 **(counts as first dc plus ch 2, now and throughout)**, turn; sc in first loop, ch 5, sc in next loop, ch 1, 3 dc in next sc, ch 1, skip next dc, sc in next dc, ch 1, 3 dc in next sc, ch 1, sc in next loop, ★ (ch 5, sc in next loop) twice, ch 1, 3 dc in next sc, ch 1, skip next dc, sc in next dc, ch 1, 3 dc in next sc, ch 1, sc in next loop; repeat from ★ across to last loop, ch 5, sc in last loop, ch 2, dc in last sc: 44 dc.

Row 3: Ch 1, turn; sc in first dc, ch 5, skip next ch-2 sp, ★ sc in next loop, ch 1, 3 dc in next sc, ch 1, skip next dc, sc in next dc, ch 5, skip next 2 ch-1 sps and next dc, sc in next dc, ch 1, 3 dc in next sc, ch 1, sc in next loop, ch 5; repeat from ★ across to last dc, sc in last dc: 42 dc.

Row 4: Ch 3 **(counts as first dc, now and throughout)**, turn; dc in same st, ch 1, sc in next loop, ch 1, ★ 3 dc in next sc, ch 1, skip next dc, sc in next dc, ch 5, sc in next loop, ch 5, skip next dc, sc in next dc, ch 1, 3 dc in next sc, ch 1, sc in next loop, ch 1; repeat from ★ across to last sc, 2 dc in last sc: 46 dc.

Row 5: Ch 1, turn; sc in first dc, ch 1, 3 dc in next sc, ch 1, skip next dc, sc in next dc, ★ ch 5, (sc in next loop, ch 5) twice, skip next dc, sc in next dc, ch 1, 3 dc in next sc, ch 1, skip next dc, sc in next dc; repeat from ★ across: 24 dc.

Row 6: Ch 3, turn; dc in same st, ch 1, skip next dc, sc in next dc, ch 1, ★ 3 dc in next sc, ch 1, sc in next loop, (ch 5, sc in next loop) twice, ch 1, 3 dc in next sc, ch 1, skip next dc, sc in next dc, ch 1; repeat from ★ across to last sc, 2 dc in last sc: 46 dc.

Continued on page 63.

Finished Size: 35" x 45"

MATERIALS

Worsted Weight Yarn:
26 ounces, (740 grams, 1,515 yards)
Crochet hook, size G (4.00 mm) **or** size
needed for gauge

GAUGE: In pattern, one repeat = 3¾" and
10 rows = 3¼"

Certificate of Quality Assurance

24K or 24KT = 24 Karat Gold

18K or 18KT = 18 Karat Gold

14K or 14KT = 14 Karat Gold

10K or 10KT = 10 Karat Gold

Sterling or 925 = Sterling Silver

Plat. = Platinum

Each piece of jewelry presented on QVC and Q2 is subject to strict standards of quality and workmanship established by our Quality Assurance Department. Through a systematic inspection program, the Quality Assurance Laboratory ensures that all the jewelry meets or exceeds those rigorous standards. The U.S. Government requires that all karat gold, sterling silver and platinum jewelry have a hallmark that accurately represents precious metal content. (See center box.) To ensure that hallmarks are accurate and comply with U.S. Government requirements, we assay samples of all karat gold, sterling silver and platinum jewelry sold by QVC.

Eric Christopher

Eric Christopher, Vice President, Quality Assurance

QVC QUALITY ASSURANCE LABORATORY
product specification • evaluation • testing • quality

QCD-5319

MILADY'S FANS

Decidedly Victorian, this elegant throw will be a thoughtful gift for Mother's Day. The afghan is graced with rows of lacy fans that are formed with double and single crochet stitches and chain spaces. The fan motif is continued in the edging, which is accented with a satin ribbon woven through an eyelet round.

Finished Size: 47" x 60"

MATERIALS
Worsted Weight Yarn:
   49 ounces, (1,390 grams, 2,860 yards)
Crochet hook, size G (4.00 mm) **or** size needed
   for gauge
Yarn needle
11 yards of ³⁄₈" wide ribbon

GAUGE: For Center, in pattern,
   10 sps (2 repeats) = 7¹⁄₂"
   11 rows = 4¹⁄₂"
   For Edging, 16 sc = 4"

CENTER

Ch 182 **loosely**.

Row 1 (Right side)**:** Sc in second ch from hook, ch 3, skip next 2 chs, sc in next ch, (ch 5, skip next 3 chs, sc in next ch) 3 times, ★ (ch 3, skip next 2 chs, sc in next ch) twice, (ch 5, skip next 3 chs, sc in next ch) 3 times; repeat from ★ across to last 3 chs, ch 3, skip next 2 chs, sc in last ch: 50 sps.

Note: Loop a short piece of yarn around any stitch to mark last row as **right** side.

Row 2: Ch 3 **(counts as first dc, now and throughout)**, turn; dc in same st, ch 3, skip next ch-3 sp, sc in next loop, 9 dc in next loop, sc in next loop, ch 3, ★ skip next ch-3 sp, 3 dc in next st, ch 3, skip next ch-3 sp, sc in next loop, 9 dc in next loop, sc in next loop, ch 3; repeat from ★ across to last ch-3 sp, skip last ch-3 sp, 2 dc in last st: 121 dc.

Row 3: Ch 1, turn; sc in first 2 dc, ch 1, skip next sc, (dc in next dc, ch 1) 9 times, ★ skip next sc, sc in next 3 dc, ch 1, skip next sc, (dc in next dc, ch 1) 9 times; repeat from ★ across to last 2 dc, skip next sc, sc in last 2 dc: 90 dc.

Row 4: Ch 1, turn; sc in first sc, ★ skip next sc, (dc in next dc, ch 1) 4 times, (dc, ch 1, dc) in next dc, (ch 1, dc in next dc) 4 times, skip next sc, sc in next sc; repeat from ★ across: 100 dc.

Row 5: Ch 6 **(counts as first dc plus ch 3)**, turn; skip first 2 dc, sc in next dc, (ch 5, skip next ch-1 sp, sc in next ch-1 sp) twice, ch 5, skip next dc, sc in next dc, ch 3, skip next 2 dc, dc in next sc, ★ ch 3, skip next 2 dc, sc in next dc, (ch 5, skip next ch-1 sp, sc in next ch-1 sp) twice, ch 5, skip next dc, sc in next dc, ch 3, skip next 2 dc, dc in next sc; repeat from ★ across: 50 sps.

Repeat Rows 2-5 until piece measures 52" from beginning ch, ending by working Row 5; do **not** finish off.

EDGING

Rnd 1: Ch 1, do **not** turn; work 208 sc evenly spaced across end of rows; sc in free loop of first ch *(Fig. 23b, page 140)*, place marker around last sc made, 2 sc in same st; working over beginning ch, work 145 sc evenly spaced across to last ch, sc in free loop of last ch, place marker around last sc made, 2 sc in same st; work 208 sc evenly spaced across end of rows; working across last row, sc in first dc, place marker around last sc made, 2 sc in same st, work 145 sc evenly spaced across to last dc, sc in last dc, place marker around last sc made, 2 sc in same st; join with slip st to first sc: 718 sc.

Note: Work in Back Loops Only throughout Edging *(Fig. 22, page 140)*.

Rnd 2 (Eyelet rnd)**:** Slip st in next sc, ch 3, dc in next sc, ch 1, ★ (skip next sc, dc in next 2 sc, ch 1) across to within 1 sc of marked sc, skip next sc, 2 dc in marked sc, ch 1, skip next sc, 2 dc in next sc, place marker around ch-1 just made, ch 1; repeat from ★ around to last sc, skip last sc; join with slip st to first dc: 484 dc.

Rnd 3: Ch 1, sc in same st, working in each ch and in each sc, sc in each st across to marked ch, 2 sc in marked ch, place marker around last sc made, sc in same st, † 2 sc in next st, sc in each st across to marked ch, 2 sc in marked ch, place marker around last sc made, sc in same st †, sc in each st across to marked ch, 2 sc in marked ch, place marker around last sc made, sc in same st, repeat from † to † once, sc in last 3 sts; join with slip st to first sc: 736 sc.

Continued on page 62.

DARLING DAISIES

Springtime showers will give you plenty of time to crochet these May flowers!
Worked as you go, the darling daisies are contrasted with rounds of blue, rose,
and yellow. The squares are assembled in strips and edged with a simple border.

Finished Size: 57" x 73"

MATERIALS
Worsted Weight Yarn:
    Ecru - 22 ounces, (620 grams, 1,445 yards)
    Yellow - 11 ounces, (310 grams, 725 yards)
    Blue - 12 ounces, (340 grams, 790 yards)
    Rose - 12 ounces, (340 grams, 790 yards)
  Crochet hook, size I (5.50 mm) **or** size needed
    for gauge
  Yarn needle

GAUGE: Each Square = 8"

SQUARE
Make 63 in the following color sequence:

	Square A	Square B
Make	32	31
Rnd 1	Yellow	Yellow
Rnd 2	Ecru	Ecru
Rnds 3-6	Blue	Rose
Rnd 7	Rose	Blue
Rnd 8	Yellow	Yellow
Rnd 9	Ecru	Ecru

Rnd 1 (Right side): With Yellow, ch 4, 11 dc in fourth ch from hook; join with slip st to top of beginning ch, finish off: 12 sts.
Note: Loop a short piece of yarn around any stitch to mark last round as **right** side.
Rnd 2: With **right** side facing, join Ecru with slip st in Front Loop Only of same st as joining *(Fig. 22, page 140)*; ch 5 **loosely**, sc in second ch from hook, dc in next 2 chs, sc in last ch **(Petal made)**, ★ slip st in Front Loop Only of next dc on Rnd 1, ch 5 **loosely**, sc in second ch from hook, dc in next 2 chs, sc in last ch; repeat from ★ around; join with slip st to first slip st, finish off: 12 Petals.

Rnd 3: With **right** side facing, working in free loops on Rnd 1 *(Fig. 23a, page 140)* and **behind** Petals, join next color with sc in any dc *(see Joining With Sc, page 140)*; sc in same st, 2 sc in each dc around; join with slip st to **both** loops of first sc: 24 sc.
Rnd 4: Ch 1, working in both loops, sc in same st, ch 1, skip next sc, hdc in next sc, (dc, ch 3, dc) in next sc, hdc in next sc, ch 1, skip next sc, ★ sc in next sc, ch 1, skip next sc, hdc in next sc, (dc, ch 3, dc) in next sc, hdc in next sc, ch 1, skip next sc; repeat from ★ around; join with slip st to first sc: 12 sps.
Rnd 5: Ch 3 **(counts as first dc, now and throughout)**, sc in tip of first Petal (in unworked ch), dc in same st on Rnd 4, ch 1, in next ch-3 sp work (dc, sc in tip of next Petal, dc, ch 3, dc, sc in tip of next Petal, dc), ch 1, ★ (dc, sc in tip of next Petal, dc) in next sc, ch 1, in next ch-3 sp work (dc, sc in tip of next Petal, dc, ch 3, dc, sc in tip of next Petal, dc), ch 1; repeat from ★ around; join with slip st to first dc.
Rnd 6: Slip st in next 2 sts and in next ch-1 sp, ch 3, 2 dc in same sp, ch 1, (3 dc, ch 3, 3 dc) in next ch-3 sp, ch 1, ★ (3 dc in next ch-1 sp, ch 1) twice, (3 dc, ch 3, 3 dc) in next ch-3 sp, ch 1; repeat from ★ 2 times **more**, 3 dc in last ch-1 sp, ch 1; join with slip st to first dc, finish off: 16 sps.
Rnd 7: With **right** side facing, join next color with slip st in any ch-3 sp; ch 3, (2 dc, ch 3, 3 dc) in same sp, ch 1, (3 dc in next ch-1 sp, ch 1) across to next ch-3 sp, ★ (3 dc, ch 3, 3 dc) in ch-3 sp, ch 1, (3 dc in next ch-1 sp, ch 1) across to next ch-3 sp; repeat from ★ around; join with slip st to first dc, finish off: 20 sps.
Rnd 8: With Yellow, repeat Rnd 7: 24 sps.
Rnd 9: With Ecru, repeat Rnd 7: 28 sps.

ASSEMBLY
Afghan is assembled by whipstitching Squares together alternating Square A and Square B, forming 4 vertical strips of 9 Squares each beginning and ending with Square A, and forming 3 vertical strips beginning and ending with Square B.

With Ecru, whipstitch Squares together beginning in center ch of first corner ch-3 and ending in center ch of next corner ch-3 *(Fig. 28a, page 142)*; then whipstitch strips together in same manner.

Continued on page 63.

LILAC LANE

Stitched in the popular mile-a-minute style, this plush afghan brings to mind an avenue of lovely lilacs. Each strip of cluster-stitch "blooms" is joined to the next by working the off-white border into the previous panel.

Finished Size: 50" x 65"

MATERIALS
Worsted Weight Yarn:
Lavender - 12 ounces, (340 grams, 760 yards)
Off-White - 30 ounces, (850 grams, 1,900 yards)
Green - 21 ounces, (600 grams, 1,330 yards)
Crochet hook, size I (5.50 mm) **or** size needed for gauge

GAUGE: 12 dc and 6 rows = 4"
Each Strip = 5" wide

STITCH GUIDE

BEGINNING CLUSTER
★ YO, insert hook in sp indicated, YO and pull up a loop, YO and draw through 2 loops on hook; repeat from ★ 2 times **more**, YO and draw through all 4 loops on hook *(Figs. 9a & b, page 137)*.

CLUSTER
★ YO, insert hook in sp indicated, YO and pull up a loop, YO and draw through 2 loops on hook; repeat from ★ 3 times **more**, YO and draw through all 5 loops on hook.

FRONT POST DOUBLE CROCHET (abbreviated FPdc)
YO, insert hook from **front** to **back** around post of st indicated, YO and pull up a loop even with last st made *(Fig. 13, page 137)*, (YO and draw through 2 loops on hook) twice.

FIRST STRIP

CENTER
With Lavender, ch 5; join with slip st to form a ring.
Row 1: Ch 2, work (beginning Cluster, ch 2, Cluster) in ring: 2 Clusters.
Row 2 (Right side): Ch 2, turn; work (beginning Cluster, ch 2, Cluster) in next ch-2 sp.
Note: Loop a short piece of yarn around any stitch to mark last row as **right** side and bottom edge.
Rows 3-60: Repeat Row 2, 58 times.
Finish off.

BORDER
Rnd 1: With **right** side facing, join Off-White with slip st in ch-2 sp at top of Center; ch 3 **(counts as first dc, now and throughout)**, place marker around last dc made for Rnd 2 joining, 10 dc in same sp; working in side of Clusters, 3 dc in each Cluster across to beginning ring, 11 dc in beginning ring; working in side of Clusters, 3 dc in each Cluster across; join with slip st to first dc, finish off: 382 dc.
Rnd 2: With **right** side facing, join Green with sc *(see Joining With Sc, page 140)* in sp **before** marked dc *(Fig. 26, page 141)*; tr in sp **before** next dc, 2 tr in sp **before** each of next 8 dc, tr in sp **before** next dc, (sc in sp **before** next 3-dc group, 7 tr in sp **before** next 3-dc group) across to next 11-dc group, sc in sp **before** next dc, tr in sp **before** next dc, 2 tr in sp **before** each of next 8 dc, tr in sp **before** next dc, (sc in sp **before** next 3-dc group, 7 tr in sp **before** next 3-dc group) across; join with slip st to first sc, finish off: 518 sts.
Rnd 3: With **wrong** side facing, join Off-White with slip st around post of any st *(Fig. 12, page 137)*; ch 3, work FPdc around next st and around each st around; join with slip st to first st, finish off.

REMAINING 9 STRIPS
Work same as First Strip through Rnd 1 of Border.
Rnd 2: With **right** side facing, join Green with sc in sp **before** marked dc, tr in sp **before** next dc, 2 tr in sp **before** each of next 8 dc, tr in sp **before** next dc, place marker around last tr made for Rnd 3 joining, (sc in sp **before** next 3-dc group, 7 tr in sp **before** next 3-dc group) across to next 11-dc group, sc in sp **before** next dc, place marker around last sc made, tr in sp **before** next dc, 2 tr in sp **before** each of next 8 dc, tr in sp **before** next dc, (sc in sp **before** next 3-dc group, 7 tr in sp **before** next 3-dc group) across; join with slip st to first sc, finish off.

Continued on page 63.

CAT'S MEOW

Fashioned in filet crochet, these country kittens are the cat's meow! Just follow our simple chart to work the feline silhouettes using easy double crochets and chain spaces. A coordinating pillow also features the "purr-fect" pattern.

MATERIALS

100% Cotton Worsted Weight Yarn:
    Afghan - 42½ ounces, (1,210 grams, 2,125 yards)
    Pillow - 10 ounces, (280 grams, 500 yards)
Crochet hook, size F (3.75 mm) **or** size needed
    for gauge
Pillow
    Fabric - ½ yard
    Polyester fiberfill
    Sewing needle and thread

GAUGE: 16 dc and 8 rows = 4"

AFGHAN

Finished Size: 45" x 71"

Ch 288 **loosely**.

Row 1 (Right side): Dc in fourth ch from hook (**3 skipped chs count as first dc**) and in each ch across: 286 dc.
Note: Loop a short piece of yarn around any stitch to mark last row as **right** side.

Row 2: Ch 3 (**counts as first dc, now and throughout**), turn; [dc in next 3 dc (**Block over Block made**)], [ch 2, skip next 2 dc, dc in next dc (**Space over Block made**)], work Block, (work Space, work Block) twice, ★ work 15 Spaces, work Block, (work Space, work Block) 3 times; repeat from ★ across.

Row 3: Ch 3, turn; work Block, [ch 2, dc in next dc (**Space over Space made**)], work Block, (work Space, work Block) twice, ★ work 15 Spaces, work Block, (work Space, work Block) 3 times, work 8 Spaces, [2 dc in ch-2 sp, dc in next dc (**Block over Space made**)], work Block, work 5 Spaces, work Block, (work Space, work Block) 3 times; repeat from ★ once **more**.

Row 4: [Turn; slip st in first 4 dc, ch 3 (**beginning decrease made**)], follow Chart across, leaving last 3 sts unworked.

Rows 5-14: Follow Chart.

Row 15: [Ch 5, turn; dc in fourth ch from hook and in next ch, dc in next dc (**beginning increase made**)], follow Chart across to last Block, work **end increase** as follows: [YO, insert hook into base of last dc made, YO and pull up a loop, YO and draw through one loop on hook, (YO and draw through 2 loops on hook) twice] 3 times.

Rows 16-23: Follow Chart.

Rows 24-89: Follow Chart Rows 2-23, 3 times.
Finish off.

Continued on page 62.

CHART

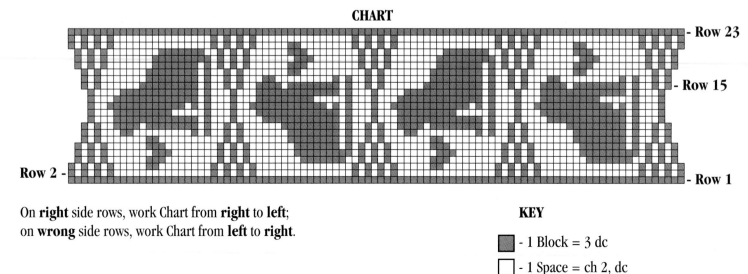

- Row 23
- Row 15
Row 2 -
- Row 1

On **right** side rows, work Chart from **right** to **left**;
on **wrong** side rows, work Chart from **left** to **right**.

KEY

▨ - 1 Block = 3 dc
☐ - 1 Space = ch 2, dc

CAT'S MEOW Continued from page 60.

PILLOW

Finished Size: 15 1/2" x 17 1/2"

Ch 72 **loosely.**

Row 1 (Right side): Dc in fourth ch from hook **(3 skipped chs count as first dc)** and in each ch across: 70 dc.

Note: Loop a short piece of yarn around any stitch to mark last row as **right** side.

Row 2: Ch 3 **(counts as first dc, now and throughout)**, turn; [dc in next 3 dc **(Block over Block made]**, work Block, [ch 2, skip next 2 dc, dc in next dc **(Space over Block made)]**, work Block, work 15 Spaces, work Block, work Space, work 2 Blocks.

Row 3: Ch 3, turn; work 2 Blocks, [ch 2, dc in next dc **(Space over Space made)]**, follow Chart across.

Row 4: Ch 3, turn; work Block, work Space, [2 dc in next ch-2 sp, dc in next dc **(Block over Space made)]**, follow Chart across.

Rows 5-31: Follow Chart.

Finish off.

Repeat for second side; do **not** finish off.

PILLOW FINISHING

Cut 2, 16" x 18" pieces of fabric. With **right** sides together and using a 1/4" seam allowance, machine-stitch around pieces, leaving an opening at bottom edge. Turn right side out. Stuff firmly with polyester fiberfill and sew final closure by hand.

Joining Rnd: With **wrong** sides together and working through **both** pieces, ch 1, sc evenly around working 3 sc in each corner and inserting pillow before closing; join with slip st to first sc, finish off.

CHART

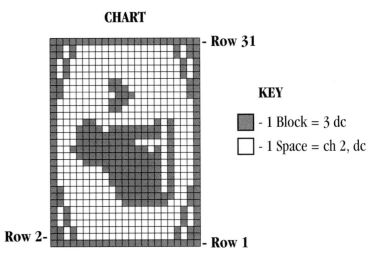

- Row 31

KEY

☒ - 1 Block = 3 dc
☐ - 1 Space = ch 2, dc

Row 2- - Row 1

On **right** side rows, work Chart from **right** to **left**;
on **wrong** side rows, work Chart from **left** to **right**.

MILADY'S FANS Continued from page 54.

Rnd 4: Ch 1, sc in same st, ★ sc in each sc across to marked sc, remove marker, 3 sc in marked sc; repeat from ★ around to last 4 sc, sc in last 4 sc; join with slip st to first sc, do **not** finish off: 744 sc.

FIRST FAN

Note: Begin working in rows.

Row 1: Do **not** turn; working in both loops, slip st in next 7 sc, ch 3, 5 dc in same st, ch 3, skip next 2 sc, sc in next sc, leave remaining sc unworked.

Row 2: Ch 3, turn; dc in next dc, (ch 1, dc in next dc) 5 times: 5 ch-1 sps.

Row 3: Ch 4, turn; (dc in next dc, ch 1) 5 times, dc in side of last sc on Row 1, ch 3, skip next 2 sc on Rnd 4 of Edging, sc in next sc, leave remaining sc unworked.

Row 4: Ch 3, turn; (dc in next dc, ch 2) 6 times, skip next ch, dc in next ch.

Row 5: Ch 3, turn; 3 dc in each of first 6 ch-2 sps, dc in next dc, ch 3, skip next 2 sc on Rnd 4 of Edging, sc in next sc, leave remaining sc unworked.

Row 6: Ch 3, turn; dc in next dc, ch 3, (skip next 3 dc, dc in sp **before** next dc, ch 3) 5 times *(Fig. 26, page 141)*, skip next 3 dc, dc in last dc.

Row 7: Ch 1, turn; (sc, dc, tr, dc, sc) in each of first 6 ch-3 sps; do **not** finish off.

NEXT 60 FANS

Row 1: Do **not** turn; skip next 2 sc on Rnd 4 of Edging, 6 dc in next sc, ch 3, skip next 2 sc in next sc, leave remaining sc unworked.

Rows 2-7: Work same as First Fan.

LAST FAN

Rows 1-6: Work same as previous Fan.

Row 7: Ch 1, turn; (sc, dc, tr, dc, sc) in each of first 6 ch-3 sps, skip last 2 sc; join with slip st to first dc on Row 1 of First Fan, finish off.

Weave ribbon through Eyelet rnd along one side of Afghan, leaving 22" at each end. Repeat for remaining three sides. Tie ends in a bow at each corner.

BABY'S KEEPSAKE Continued from page 52.

Row 7: Ch 1, turn; sc in first dc, ch 5, skip next 2 ch-1 sps and next dc, sc in next dc, ★ ch 1, 3 dc in next sc, ch 1, sc in next loop, ch 5, sc in next loop, ch 1, 3 dc in next sc, ch 1, skip next dc, sc in next dc, ch 5, skip next 2 ch-1 sps and next dc, sc in next dc; repeat from ★ across: 42 dc.

Row 8: Ch 5, turn; sc in first loop, ★ ch 5, skip next dc, sc in next dc, ch 1, 3 dc in next sc, ch 1, sc in next loop, ch 1, 3 dc in next sc, ch 1, skip next dc, sc in next dc, ch 5, sc in next loop; repeat from ★ across to last sc, ch 2, dc in last sc: 44 dc.

Row 9: Ch 1, turn; sc in first dc, ch 5, skip next ch-2 sp, sc in next loop, ch 5, skip next dc, sc in next dc, ch 1, 3 dc in next sc, ch 1, skip next dc, sc in next dc, ch 5, ★ (sc in next loop, ch 5) twice, skip next dc, sc in next dc, ch 1, 3 dc in next sc, ch 1, skip next dc, sc in next dc, ch 5; repeat from ★ across to last 2 sps, sc in next loop, ch 5, skip last ch-2 sp, sc in last dc: 21 dc.
Repeat Rows 2-9 until Center measures 36³/4" from beginning ch, ending by working Row 9.
Do **not** finish off.

EDGING

Rnd 1: Ch 4 (**counts as first tr, now and throughout**), do **not** turn; tr in last sc on last row; work 193 tr evenly spaced across end of rows; working in free loops of beginning ch **(Fig. 23b, page 140)**, 2 tr in first ch, work 133 tr evenly spaced across to next corner, 2 tr in corner ch; work 193 tr evenly spaced across end of rows; working in Back Loops Only across last row **(Fig. 22, page 140)**, 2 tr in first sc, work 133 tr evenly spaced across; join with slip st to first tr: 660 tr.

Rnd 2: Ch 3, dc in next tr, ch 2, skip next tr, sc in next tr, ch 2, skip next tr, ★ dc in next 2 tr, ch 2, skip next tr, sc in next tr, ch 2, skip next tr; repeat from ★ around; join with slip st to first dc: 264 dc.

Rnd 3: Ch 3, dc in same st, ch 4, 2 dc in next dc, ch 4, † (dc in next 2 dc, ch 4) 38 times, (2 dc in next dc, ch 4) twice, (dc in next 2 dc, ch 4) 26 times †, (2 dc in next dc, ch 4) twice, repeat from † to † once; join with slip st to first dc: 272 dc.

Rnd 4: Ch 3, dc in next dc, ch 2, sc in next ch-4 sp, ch 2, (dc in next 2 dc, ch 2, sc in next ch-4 sp, ch 2) around; join with slip st to first dc.

Rnd 5: Ch 4, tr in next dc, ch 5, 2 tr in next sc, ch 5, (tr in next 2 dc, ch 5) 40 times, 2 tr in next sc, ch 5, (tr in next 2 dc, ch 5) 28 times, 2 tr in next sc, ch 5, (tr in next 2 dc, ch 5) 40 times, 2 tr in next sc, ch 5, (tr in next 2 dc, ch 5) 27 times; join with slip st to first tr: 280 tr.

Rnd 6: Ch 3, dc in next tr, ch 3, sc in next loop, ch 3, ★ dc in next 2 tr, ch 3, sc in next loop, ch 3; repeat from ★ around; join with slip st to first dc.

Rnd 7: Ch 4, tr in next dc, ch 5, (tr in next 2 dc, ch 5) around; join with slip st to first tr.

Rnd 8: Ch 3, dc in next tr, ch 3, sc in next loop, ch 3, ★ dc in next 2 tr, ch 3, sc in next loop, ch 3; repeat from ★ around; join with slip st to first dc.

Rnd 9: Ch 3, dc in next dc, ch 3, slip st in next sc, ch 3, ★ dc in next 2 dc, ch 3, slip st in next sc, ch 3; repeat from ★ around; join with slip st to first dc, finish off.

LILAC LANE Continued from page 58.

Rnd 3 (Joining rnd): With **wrong** side facing, join Off-White with slip st around marked tr; ch 3, work FPdc around next st and around each st around to marked sc, work FPdc around marked sc and around next 3 tr, ch 1; place Strips with **right** sides together and bottom edges at same end, slip st in corresponding FPdc on **previous Strip**, (work FPdc around next tr on **new Strip**, ch 1, slip st in next FPdc on **previous Strip**) twice, ★ work FPdc around next 6 sts on **new Strip**, ch 1, skip next 5 FPdc on **previous Strip**, slip st in next FPdc, (work FPdc around next tr on **new Strip**, ch 1, slip st in next FPdc on **previous Strip**) twice; repeat from ★ across to last 3 sts on **new Strip**, work FPdc around last 3 sts; join with slip st to first st, finish off.

DARLING DAISIES Continued from page 56.

EDGING

Rnd 1: With **right** side facing, join Ecru with sc in any corner ch-3 sp; ch 2, sc in same sp, ★ † ch 1, skip next dc, sc in next dc, ch 1, (sc in next ch-1 sp, ch 1, skip next dc, sc in next dc, ch 1) 6 times, [(sc in next ch-sp, ch 1) twice, skip next dc, sc in next dc, ch 1, (sc in next ch-1 sp, ch 1, skip next dc, sc in next dc, ch 1) 6 times] across to next corner ch-3 sp †, (sc, ch 2, sc) in ch-3 sp; repeat from ★ 2 times **more**, then repeat from † to † once; join with slip st to first sc.

Rnd 2: Slip st in first ch-2 sp, ch 1, (sc, ch 2, sc) in same sp, ch 1, (sc in next ch-1 sp, ch 1) across to next ch-2 sp, ★ (sc, ch 2, sc) in ch-2 sp, ch 1, (sc in next ch-1 sp, ch 1) across to next ch-2 sp; repeat from ★ around; join with slip st to first sc.

Rnd 3: (Slip st, ch 1) twice in first ch-2 sp, (slip st in next ch-1 sp, ch 1) across to next ch-2 sp, ★ (slip st, ch 1) twice in ch-2 sp, (slip st in next ch-1 sp, ch 1) across to next ch-2 sp; repeat from ★ around; join with slip st to first slip st, finish off.

FATHER'S FAVORITE

This manly throw will be Dad's favorite catch on Father's Day!
Clusters and front post double crochet stitches lend robust texture
to the wrap, which is edged with reverse single crochets.

Finished Size: 52" x 71"

MATERIALS
Worsted Weight Yarn:
71 ounces,
(2,020 grams, 4,465 yards)
Crochet hook, size I (5.50 mm) **or** size
needed for gauge

GAUGE: 13 sc and 14 rows = 4"

Ch 60 **loosely**.
Rnd 1 (Right side)**:** Sc in second ch from hook and in each ch across to last ch, 3 sc in last ch; working in free loops of beginning ch **(Fig. 23b, page 140)**, sc in next 57 chs, 2 sc in same st as first sc; join with slip st to first sc: 120 sc.
Note #1: Work in Back Loops Only throughout **(Fig. 22, page 140)**, unless otherwise indicated.
Note #2: To work **Front Post double crochet (abbreviated FPdc)**, YO, insert hook from **front** to **back** around post of st indicated, YO and pull up a loop **(Fig. 13, page 137)**, (YO and draw through 2 loops on hook) twice.
Rnd 2: Ch 1, 2 sc in same st, † sc in next 7 sc, work FPdc around next sc, (sc in next 13 sc, work FPdc around next sc) 3 times, sc in next 7 sc, 3 sc in next sc †, sc in next sc, 3 sc in next sc, repeat from † to † once, sc in last sc and in same st as first sc; join with slip st to first sc: 128 sts.
Rnds 3-8: Ch 1, 2 sc in same st, † sc in each sc across to next FPdc, (work FPdc around next FPdc, sc in each sc across to next FPdc) across to last FPdc **before** next corner 3-sc group, work FPdc around last FPdc †, (sc in each sc across to center sc of next corner 3-sc group, 3 sc in center sc) twice, repeat from † to † once, sc in each sc across to center sc of next corner 3-sc group, 3 sc in center sc, sc in each sc across and in same st as first sc; join with slip st to first sc: 176 sts.
Note: To work **Cluster**, YO, insert hook in **both** loops of next st, YO and pull up a loop, YO and draw through 2 loops on hook, ★ YO, insert hook in **same** st, YO and pull up a loop, YO and draw through 2 loops on hook; repeat from ★ 3 times **more**, YO and draw through all 6 loops on hook **(Figs. 9a & b, page 137)**.
Rnd 9: Ch 1, 2 sc in same st, † (work Cluster, sc in each sc across to next FPdc) across to last FPdc **before** next corner, ★ work Cluster, sc in each sc across to next corner 3-sc group, work Cluster, 3 sc in center sc †; repeat from ★ once **more**, then repeat from † to † once, work Cluster, sc in each sc across to last sc, work Cluster, sc in same st as first sc; join with slip st to first sc: 184 sts.

Continued on page 73.

64

BRIDE'S LACE

Present a June bride with "something blue" — our genteel afghan! The blue panels are fashioned with rows of cluster stitches and accented with lacy motifs. A latticework border connects the lush fringe.

Finished Size: 45" x 65"

MATERIALS
Worsted Weight Yarn:
    Blue - 28 ounces, (800 grams, 1,920 yards)
    White - 15 ounces, (430 grams, 1,030 yards)
Crochet hook, size H (5.00 mm) **or** size needed
    for gauge
Yarn needle

GAUGE: Center of Motif = 4¹/₂"
                Center Section: In pattern,
                (Cluster, ch 1) 7 times and 6 rows = 4"

END PANEL (Make 2)
STRIP
FIRST MOTIF
Center
With White, ch 26 **loosely**.
Row 1 (Right side)**:** Dc in eighth ch from hook, (ch 2, skip next 2 chs, dc in next ch) across: 7 sps.
Note: Loop a short piece of yarn around any stitch to mark last row as **right** side.
Rows 2-8: Ch 5, turn; (dc in next dc, ch 2) 6 times, skip next 2 chs, dc in next ch.

Edging
Rnd 1: Ch 1, turn; 2 sc in first ch-2 sp, † (ch 1, 2 sc in next sp) 4 times, ch 5 **loosely**, **turn**; skip first 2 sc, (dc, ch 5 **loosely**, dc) in next sc, ch 5 **loosely**, skip next ch-1 sp, slip st in next ch-1 sp, **turn**; slip st in first 8 sts, (slip st, ch 3, slip st) in next ch, slip st in next 8 sts, 2 sc in next sp, ch 1, (2 sc, ch 3, 2 sc) in next sp, ch 1, 2 sc in next sp, ch 1, sc in next sp, ch 1, (2 sc in next sp, ch 1) twice, sc in next sp, ch 5 **loosely**, **turn**; skip first ch-1 sp, (dc, ch 5 **loosely**, dc) in next ch-1 sp, ch 5 **loosely**, skip next ch-1 sp, slip st in next ch-1 sp, turn; slip st in first 8 sts, (slip st, ch 3, slip st) in next ch, slip st in next 8 sts, 2 sc in next sp, ch 1 †, (2 sc, ch 3, 2 sc) in next sp, repeat from † to † once, 2 sc in same sp as first sc, ch 3; join with slip st to first sc.

Rnd 2: Turn; slip st in first ch-3 sp, ★ † ch 8 **loosely**, skip next 8 sts, slip st in ch in front of next slip st *(Fig. 1)*, ch 10 **loosely**, slip st in next ch-3 sp, ch 10 **loosely**, skip next 5 slip sts, slip st in ch in front of next slip st, ch 8 **loosely** †, slip st in next ch-3 sp; repeat from ★ 2 times **more**, then repeat from † to † once; join with slip st to first slip st: 144 chs.

Fig. 1

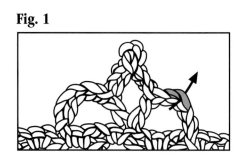

Note: For markers, 3 different colors are recommended, using the same color for each type of joining specified.
Rnd 3: Turn; slip st in first 50 chs, place marker around last ch worked **into** for joining placement, slip st in next 9 chs, place marker around last ch worked **into** for st placement, slip st in next 63 chs, place marker around last ch worked **into** for Border placement, slip st in next 9 chs, place marker around last ch worked **into** for st placement, slip st in each ch around; join with slip st to first slip st, finish off.

REMAINING FIVE MOTIFS
Work same as First Motif through Rnd 2 of Edging.
Rnd 3 (Joining rnd)**:** Turn; slip st in first 50 chs, place marker around last ch worked **into** for joining placement, slip st in next 9 chs, place marker around last ch worked **into** for st placement, slip st in next 36 chs, holding Motifs with **wrong** sides together, slip st in ch marked for joining placement on **previous Motif** *(Fig. 25, page 140)*, remove marker, slip st in next 10 chs on **new Motif**, skip next 9 slip sts on **previous Motif**, slip st in ch in front of next slip st, slip st in next 6 chs on **new Motif**, skip next 6 slip sts on **previous Motif**, slip st in ch in front of next slip st, slip st in next 10 chs on **new Motif**, skip next 9 slip sts on **previous Motif**, slip st in ch in front of next slip st, slip st in next 10 chs on **new Motif**, place marker around last ch worked into for st placement, slip st in each ch around on **new Motif**; join with slip st to first slip st, finish off.

Continued on page 74.

ROSES REMEMBERED

Wrap up in beautiful blooms to commemorate National Rose Month!
The center "trellis" is formed with delicate squares, each marked with an
"X" of cluster stitches. A border of dimensional roses, which are worked
into the lacy blocks as you go, is finished with a picot edging.

Finished Size: 47" x 61"

MATERIALS

Worsted Weight Yarn:
    57 ounces, (1,620 grams, 3,590 yards)
Crochet hook, size I (5.50 mm) **or** size needed
    for gauge

GAUGE: Each Square = 7"

STITCH GUIDE

BEGINNING CLUSTER
Ch 2, ★ YO, insert hook in sp indicated, YO and pull up a
loop, YO and draw through 2 loops on hook; repeat from
★ once **more**, YO and draw through all 3 loops on hook
***(Figs. 9a & b, page 137)*.**
CLUSTER
★ YO, insert hook in sp indicated, YO and pull up a loop,
YO and draw through 2 loops on hook; repeat from ★
2 times **more**, YO and draw through all 4 loops on hook.
PICOT
Slip st in third ch from hook.

SOLID SQUARE (Make 24)

Ch 4; join with slip st to form a ring.
Rnd 1 (Right side)**:** Ch 1, (sc in ring, ch 3) 4 times; join with
slip st to first sc: 4 ch-3 sps.
Note: Loop a short piece of yarn around any stitch to mark last
round as **right** side.
Rnd 2: Slip st in first ch-3 sp, work (beginning Cluster, ch 3,
Cluster) in same sp, ch 3, work (Cluster, ch 3) twice in next
ch-3 sp and in each ch-3 sp around; join with slip st to top of
beginning Cluster: 8 ch-3 sps.
Rnd 3: Slip st in first ch-3 sp, work (beginning Cluster, ch 3,
Cluster) in same sp, ch 2, 4 dc in next ch-3 sp, ch 2, ★ work
(Cluster, ch 3, Cluster) in next ch-3 sp, ch 2, 4 dc in next
ch-3 sp, ch 2; repeat from ★ around; join with slip st to top of
beginning Cluster.

Rnds 4 and 5: Slip st in first ch-3 sp, work (beginning Cluster,
ch 3, Cluster) in same sp, ch 2, 2 dc in next ch-2 sp, dc in next
dc and in each dc across to next ch-2 sp, 2 dc in ch-2 sp, ch 2,
★ work (Cluster, ch 3, Cluster) in next ch-3 sp, ch 2, 2 dc in
next ch-2 sp, dc in next dc and in each dc across to next
ch-2 sp, 2 dc in next ch-2 sp, ch 2; repeat from ★ around; join
with slip st to top of beginning Cluster.
Finish off.

ROSE SQUARE (Make 24)

Ch 4; join with slip st to form a ring.
Rnd 1 (Right side)**:** Ch 1, (sc in ring, ch 3) 6 times; join with
slip st to first sc: 6 ch-3 sps.
Note: Mark last round as **right** side.
Rnd 2: Slip st in first ch-3 sp, ch 1, (sc, 3 dc, sc) in same sp
and in each ch-3 sp around; join with slip st to first sc: 6 Petals.
Rnd 3: Ch 1, working **behind** Petals, sc around post of first sc
on Rnd 1 *(Fig. 12, page 137)*, ch 4, (sc around post of next
sc on Rnd 1, ch 4) 5 times; join with slip st to first sc:
6 ch-4 sps.
Rnd 4: Slip st in first ch-4 sp, ch 1, (sc, 5 dc, sc) in same sp
and in each ch-4 sp around; join with slip st to first sc:
6 Petals.
Rnd 5: Ch 1, working **behind** Petals, sc around post of first sc
on Rnd 3, ch 5, (sc around post of next sc on Rnd 3, ch 5) 5
times; join with slip st to first sc: 6 ch-5 sps.
Rnd 6: Slip st in first ch-5 sp, ch 1, (sc, 7 dc, sc) in same sp
and in each ch-5 sp around; join with slip st to first sc: 6 Petals.
Rnd 7: Ch 1, working **behind** Petals, sc around post of first sc
on Rnd 5, ch 5, (sc around post of next sc on Rnd 5, ch 5) 5
times; join with slip st to first sc: 6 ch-5 sps.
Rnd 8: Slip st in first ch-5 sp, ch 1, (sc, ch 5) twice in same sp
and in each ch-5 sp around; join with slip st to first sc:
12 ch-5 sps.
Rnd 9: Slip st in first ch-5 sp, work (beginning Cluster, ch 3,
Cluster) in same sp, ch 5, work Picot, ch 2, sc in next ch-5 sp,
ch 7, sc in next ch-5 sp, ch 5, work Picot, ch 2, ★ work
(Cluster, ch 3, Cluster) in next ch-5 sp, ch 5, work Picot, ch 2,
sc in next ch-5 sp, ch 7, sc in next ch-5 sp, ch 5, work Picot,
ch 2; repeat from ★ around; join with slip st to top of beginning
Cluster.

Continued on page 75.

WEDDING RING

Delight a newly married couple with this afghan reminiscent of the traditional Double Wedding Ring quilt. The pattern of interlocking rings is formed with several motifs, including ovals, large lacy squares, and small setting squares. The wrap is completed with dainty scallops.

Finished Size: 53" x 72"

MATERIALS

Worsted Weight Yarn:
White - 36 ounces, (1,020 grams, 2,100 yards)
Rose - 18 ounces, (510 grams, 1,050 yards)
Green - 15 ounces, (430 grams, 875 yards)
Crochet hook, size G (4.00 mm) **or** size needed for gauge

GAUGE: 16 dc and 5 rows = 4"

OVAL (Make 82)

CENTER

With White, ch 23 **loosely**.

Rnd 1 (Right side): (Sc, ch 3) 4 times in second ch from hook, (skip next 2 chs, sc in next ch, ch 3) across to last 3 chs, skip next 2 chs, (sc, ch 3) 4 times in last ch; working in free loops of beginning ch *(Fig. 23b, page 140)*, skip next 2 chs, sc in next ch, (ch 3, skip next 2 chs, sc in next ch) across to last 2 chs, skip last 2 chs, ch 1, hdc in first sc to form last sp: 20 sps.

Note: Loop a short piece of yarn around any stitch to mark last round as **right** side.

Rnd 2: Ch 1, sc in same sp, ch 3, sc in next ch-3 sp, ch 3, (sc, ch 3) twice in next ch-3 sp, (sc in next ch-3 sp, ch 3) 9 times, (sc, ch 3) twice in next ch-3 sp, (sc in next ch-3 sp, ch 3) across; join with slip st to first sc, finish off: 22 ch-3 sps.

BORDER

FIRST SECTION

Row 1: With **right** side of Center facing, join Rose with slip st in last ch-3 sp worked; ch 3 **(counts as first dc, now and throughout)**, 2 dc in same sp, 2 dc in each of next 3 ch-3 sps: 9 dc.

Row 2: Ch 1, turn; sc in each dc across.

Row 3: Ch 1, turn; sc in first sc, (ch 3, skip next sc, sc in next sc) 4 times; do **not** finish off: 4 ch-3 sps.

SECOND SECTION

Row 1: Slip st in end of next row, slip st 3 times in next row, slip st in same ch-3 sp on Rnd 2 of Center as last dc of Row 1 of First Section, ch 3, 2 dc in same sp, 2 dc in each of next 3 ch-3 sps: 9 dc.

Row 2: Ch 1, turn; sc in each dc across.

Row 3: Ch 1, turn; sc in first sc, (ch 3, skip next sc, sc in next sc) 4 times; finish off: 4 ch-3 sps.

THIRD SECTION

Row 1: With **right** side of Center facing, join Green with slip st in next ch-3 sp on Center; ch 3, 2 dc in same sp, 2 dc in each of next 3 ch-3 sps: 9 dc.

Row 2: Ch 1, turn; sc in each dc across; join with slip st to Row 2 on previous section.

Row 3: Turn; sc in first sc, (ch 3, skip next sc, sc in next sc) 4 times; finish off: 4 ch-3 sps.

FOURTH SECTION

Row 1: With **right** side of Center facing, join Rose with slip st in next ch-3 sp on Center; ch 3, 2 dc in same sp, 2 dc in each of next 3 ch-3 sps: 9 dc.

Row 2: Ch 1, turn; sc in each dc across; join with slip st to Row 2 on previous section.

Row 3: Turn; sc in first sc, (ch 3, skip next sc, sc in next sc) 4 times; do **not** finish off: 4 ch-3 sps.

FIFTH SECTION

Row 1: Slip st in end of next row, slip st 3 times in next row, slip st in same ch-3 sp as last dc of Row 1 of Fourth Section, ch 3, 2 dc in same sp, 2 dc in each of next 3 ch-3 sps: 9 dc.

Row 2: Ch 1, turn; sc in each dc across.

Row 3: Ch 1, turn; sc in first sc, (ch 3, skip next sc, sc in next sc) 4 times; finish off: 4 ch-3 sps.

SIXTH SECTION

Row 1: With **right** side of Center facing, join Green with slip st in next ch-3 sp on Center; ch 3, 2 dc in same sp, 2 dc in each of next 3 ch-3 sps; join with slip st to Row 2 on First Section: 9 dc.

Row 2: Turn; sc in each dc across; join with slip st to Row 2 on previous section.

Row 3: Turn; sc in first sc, (ch 3, skip next sc, sc in next sc) 4 times; finish off.

Continued on page 72.

LARGE SQUARE (Make 35)

With White, ch 4; join with slip st to form a ring.

Rnd 1: Ch 1, sc in ring, (ch 3, sc in ring) 7 times, ch 1, hdc in first sc to form last sp: 8 sps.

Rnd 2: Ch 1, sc in same sp, (ch 3, sc in next ch-3 sp) around, ch 1, hdc in first sc to form last sp.

Rnd 3: Ch 1, sc in same sp, ch 3, sc in next ch-3 sp, ch 3, ★ (sc, ch 5, sc) in next ch-3 sp, ch 3, sc in next ch-3 sp, ch 3; repeat from ★ around, sc in first ch-3 sp, ch 2, dc in first sc to form last loop: 12 sc.

Rnd 4: Ch 1, sc in same sp, ch 3, (sc in next ch-3 sp, ch 3) twice, ★ (sc, ch 5, sc) in next loop, ch 3, (sc in next ch-3 sp, ch 3) twice; repeat from ★ around, sc in first loop, ch 2, dc in first sc to form last loop: 16 sc.

Rnd 5: Ch 3, dc in same sp, 3 dc in next ch-3 sp, sc in next ch-3 sp, 3 dc in next ch-3 sp, ★ (2 dc, ch 3, 2 dc) in next loop, 3 dc in next ch-3 sp, sc in next ch-3 sp, 3 dc in next ch-3 sp; repeat from ★ around, 2 dc in same loop as first dc, ch 1, hdc in first dc to form last sp: 40 dc.

Rnd 6: Ch 3, dc in same sp and in next 11 sts, ★ (2 dc, ch 3, 2 dc) in next ch-3 sp, dc in next 11 sts; repeat from ★ around, 2 dc in same ch-3 sp as first dc, ch 1, hdc in first dc to form last sp: 60 dc.

Rnd 7: Ch 3, dc in same sp and in each dc across to next corner ch-3 sp, ★ (2 dc, ch 3, 2 dc) in ch-3 sp, dc in each dc across to next corner ch-3 sp; repeat from ★ around, 2 dc in same ch-3 sp as first dc, ch 1, hdc in first dc to form last sp; do **not** finish off: 76 dc.

Rnd 8 (Joining rnd): Ch 1, sc in same sp, ch 1, holding **Oval** with **wrong** sides together, skip first ch-3 sp on **Oval**, sc in next ch-3 sp *(Fig. 25, page 140)*, ch 1, † skip next dc on **Large Square**, sc in next dc, ch 1, sc in next ch-3 sp on **Oval**, ch 1 †, repeat from † to † across to last ch-3 sp on **Oval**, sc in next ch-3 sp on **Large Square**, ch 5, sc in last ch-3 sp on **Oval**; ★ with **right** side of next **Oval** facing, sc in first ch-3 sp, ch 5, sc in same ch-3 sp on **Large Square**, ch 1, sc in next ch-3 sp on **Oval**, ch 1, repeat from † to † across to last ch-3 sp on **Oval**, sc in next ch-3 sp on **Large Square**, ch 5, sc in last ch-3 sp on **Oval**; repeat from ★ 2 times **more**, sc in skipped ch-3 sp on first **Oval**, ch 5; join with slip st to first sc, finish off.

Note: Continue to join in same manner forming 5 vertical strips of 7 Large Squares each.

SMALL SQUARES

CORNER SQUARE (Make 4)

With Green, ch 4; join with slip st to form a ring.

Rnd 1: Ch 1, (sc in ring, ch 3) 4 times; join with slip st to first sc: 4 sps.

Rnd 2: Slip st in first ch-3 sp, ch 3, (dc, ch 2, 2 dc) in same sp, ch 1, ★ (2 dc, ch 2, 2 dc) in next ch-3 sp, ch 1; repeat from ★ around; join with slip st to first dc.

Rnd 3 (Joining rnd): Ch 4, (2 dc, ch 2, 2 dc) in next corner ch-2 sp, ch 1, skip next dc, dc in next dc and in next ch-1 sp, dc in next dc, ch 1, (2 dc, ch 2, 2 dc) in next corner ch-2 sp, holding Afghan with **wrong** sides together and working in end of each center row on Borders, † sc in Border on corner **Oval** (center row), skip next dc on **Corner Square**, dc in next dc and in next ch-1 sp, dc in next dc, sc in next Border on same **Oval** †, 2 dc in next ch-2 sp on **Corner Square**, ch 1, sc in loop between joining sc on **Large Square**, ch 1, 2 dc in same ch-2 sp on **Corner Square**, repeat from † to † once, (2 dc, ch 2, 2 dc) in next corner ch-2 sp on **Corner Square**, ch 1, skip next dc, dc in next dc and in next ch-1 sp; join with slip st to third ch of beginning ch-4, finish off.

SIDE SQUARE (Make 20)

Work same as Corner Square through Rnd 2.

Rnd 3 (Joining rnd): Ch 4, (2 dc, ch 2, 2 dc) in next corner ch-2 sp, holding Afghan with **wrong** sides together and working in end of each center row on Borders, sc in corresponding Border on first **Oval** (center row), skip next dc on **Side Square**, dc in next dc and in next ch-1 sp, dc in next dc, sc in next Border on same **Oval**, ★ 2 dc in next corner ch-2 sp on **Side Square**, ch 1, sc in loop between joining sc on **Large Square**, ch 1, 2 dc in same ch-2 sp on **Side Square**, sc in first Border on next **Oval**, skip next dc on **Side Square**, dc in next dc and in next ch-1 sp, dc in next dc, sc in next Border on same **Oval**; repeat from ★ once **more**, (2 dc, ch 2, 2 dc) in next corner ch-2 sp on **Side Square**, ch 1, skip next dc, dc in next dc and in next ch-1 sp; join with slip st to third ch of beginning ch-4, finish off.

FILL-IN SQUARE (Make 24)

Work same as Corner Square through Rnd 2.

Rnd 3 (Joining rnd): Ch 3, holding Afghan with **wrong** sides together and working in end of each center row on Borders, sc in corresponding Border on any **Oval** (center row), ★ † 2 dc in next ch-2 sp on **Fill-in Square**, ch 1, sc in loop between joining sc on **Large Square**, ch 1, 2 dc in same ch-2 sp on **Fill-in Square**, sc in corresponding Border on next **Oval**, skip next dc on **Fill-in Square**, dc in next dc and in next ch-1 sp †, dc in next dc, sc in next Border on same **Oval**; repeat from ★ 2 times **more**, then repeat from † to † once; join with slip st to first dc, finish off.

EDGING

With **right** side facing, using White and beginning in any corner ch-2 sp, ★ (slip st, ch 3, 2 dc) in corner ch-2 sp, (slip st, ch 3, 2 dc) in each of next 2 ch-1 sps, (slip st, ch 3, 2 dc) in next ch-2 sp, skip first ch-3 sp on next **Oval**, (slip st, ch 3, 2 dc) in each of next 10 ch-3 sps, skip next ch-3 sp, † (slip st, ch 3, 2 dc) in next ch-2 sp on **Side Square**, skip next ch-1 sp and next dc, (slip st, ch 3, 2 dc) in next dc, (slip st, ch 3, 2 dc) in next ch-2 sp, skip first ch-3 sp on next **Oval**, (slip st, ch 3, 2 dc) in each of next 10 ch-3 sps, skip next ch-3 sp †, repeat from † to † across to next **Corner Square**, (slip st, ch 3, 2 dc) in next ch-2 sp, (slip st, ch 3, 2 dc) in each of next 2 ch-1 sps; repeat from ★ around; join with slip st in first ch-2 sp, finish off.

FATHER'S FAVORITE Continued from page 64.

Rnd 10: Ch 1, 2 sc in same st, ★ sc in each st across to center sc of next corner 3-sc group, 3 sc in center sc; repeat from ★ 2 times **more**, sc in each st across and in same st as first sc; join with slip st to first sc: 192 sc.

Rnd 11: Ch 1, 2 sc in same st, sc in next 2 sc, † work FPdc around next sc, sc in next sc, work Cluster, sc in next 9 sc, work Cluster, sc in next sc †, repeat from † to † across to within 2 sc of next corner 3-sc group, work FPdc around next sc, ★ sc in next 2 sc, 3 sc in center sc, sc in next 2 sc, repeat from † to † across to within 2 sc of next corner 3-sc group, work FPdc around next sc; repeat from ★ 2 times **more**, sc in each sc across and in same st as first sc; join with slip st to first sc: 200 sts.

Rnd 12: Ch 1, 2 sc in same st, ★ † sc in each sc across to next FPdc, (work FPdc around next FPdc, sc in each st across to next FPdc) across to last FPdc **before** next corner 3-sc group, work FPdc around last FPdc †, sc in each sc across to center sc of next corner 3-sc group, 3 sc in center sc; repeat from ★ 2 times **more**, then repeat from † to † once, sc in each sc across and in same st as first sc; join with slip st to first sc: 208 sts.

Rnd 13: Ch 1, 2 sc in same st, sc in each sc across to next FPdc, † work FPdc around next FPdc, sc in next 3 sc, work Cluster, (sc in next 2 sc, work Cluster) twice, sc in next 3 sc †, repeat from † to † across to last FPdc **before** next corner 3-sc group, work FPdc around last FPdc, ★ sc in each sc across to center sc of next corner 3-sc group, 3 sc in center sc, sc in each sc across to next FPdc, repeat from † to † across to last FPdc **before** next corner 3-sc group, work FPdc around last FPdc; repeat from ★ 2 times **more**, sc in each sc across and in same st as first sc; join with slip st to first sc: 216 sts.

Rnds 14-22: Repeat Rnd 12, 9 times: 288 sts.

Rnd 23: Ch 1, 2 sc in same st, work Cluster, ★ † sc in each sc across to next FPdc, (work Cluster, sc in each sc across to next FPdc) across to last FPdc **before** next corner 3-sc group, work Cluster, sc in each sc across to next corner 3-sc group, work Cluster †, 3 sc in center sc, work Cluster; repeat from ★ 2 times **more**, then repeat from † to † once, sc in same st as first sc; join with slip st to first sc: 296 sts.

Rnds 24-91: Repeat Rnds 10-23, 4 times; then repeat Rnds 10-21 once **more**: 840 sts.

Rnd 92: Ch 1, working from **left** to **right**, work reverse sc in both loops of each st around *(Figs. 17a-d, page 138)*; join with slip st to first st, finish off.

BRIDE'S LACE Continued from page 66.

BORDER

Note: To work **double treble crochet (abbreviated dtr)**, YO 3 times, insert hook in st or sp indicated, YO and pull up a loop, (YO and draw through 2 loops on hook) 4 times *(Figs. 8a & b, page 136)*.

Row 1: With **right** side of Strip facing, join Blue with slip st in ch marked for Border placement, remove marker; ch 4 **(counts as first dc plus ch 1, now and throughout)**, tr in fourth ch from hook, ch 1, ★ † sc in next marked ch, remove marker, ch 2, skip next 5 slip sts, dc in ch behind next slip st, ch 1, dc in base of dc just made, ch 2, skip next 4 slip sts, sc in ch behind next slip st, ch 1, skip next 2 slip sts, hdc in ch behind next slip st, ch 1, skip next 2 slip sts, sc in ch behind next slip st, ch 2, skip next 4 slip sts, dc in ch behind next slip st, ch 1, hdc in base of dc just made, ch 2, skip next 4 slip sts, sc in ch behind next slip st, ch 1 †, dtr in next joining, ch 1, tr in base of dtr just made, (ch 1, tr, ch 1, dtr) in same st; repeat from ★ 4 times **more**, then repeat from † to † once, skip next 8 slip sts, tr in ch behind next slip st, ch 1, dc in base of tr just made: 77 sps.

Row 2: Ch 4, turn; (YO, insert hook in **next** sp, YO and pull up a loop, YO and draw through 2 loops on hook) twice, YO and draw through all 3 loops on hook, ch 1, ★ YO, insert hook in same sp as last half of last st, YO and pull up a loop, YO and draw through 2 loops on hook, YO, insert hook in next sp, YO and pull up a loop, YO and draw through 2 loops on hook, YO and draw through all 3 loops on hook, ch 1; repeat from ★ across to last dc, dc in last dc.

Note: To work **Cluster**, YO, insert hook in **same** st, YO and pull up a loop, YO and draw through 2 loops on hook, skip next ch, YO, insert hook in next st, YO and pull up a loop, YO and draw through 2 loops on hook, YO and draw through all 3 loops on hook *(Figs. 9a & b, page 137)*.

Rows 3-13: Ch 3 **(counts as first hdc plus ch 1)**, turn; work Cluster, (ch 1, work Cluster) across: 77 Clusters. Finish off.

TRIM

Row 1: With **right** side of Border facing, skip first ch-1 sp on Row 13 and join White with slip st in next Cluster; ch 1, sc in same st, ★ [ch 1, sc in back ridge of ch just made *(Fig. 2b, page 135)*] 3 times, skip next 2 ch-1 sps, sc in next Cluster; repeat from ★ across: 38 loops.

Row 2: Turn; (ch 1, sc in back ridge of ch just made) 3 times, sc in center sc of first loop, ★ (ch 1, sc in back ridge of ch just made) 3 times, sc in center sc of next loop; repeat from ★ across, ch 1, sc in back ridge of ch just made, tr in last sc to form last loop: 39 loops.

Row 3: Ch 1, turn; sc in same st, ★ (ch 1, sc in back ridge of ch just made) 3 times, sc in center sc of next loop; repeat from ★ across.

Row 4: Repeat Row 2; finish off.

CENTER SECTION

FIRST END

Joining in ch marked for joining placement, work same as Border of End Panel through Row 3.

Rows 4-49: Repeat Row 3, 46 times. Finish off.

SECOND END

Working across remaining End Panel and joining in ch marked for joining placement, work same as Border of End Panel through Row 2. Finish off.

ASSEMBLY

With Blue, whipstitch last rows of Center Sections together *(Fig. 28a, page 142)*.

Holding six strands of White together, add fringe in each loop of Trim *(Figs. 29a & c, page 142)*.

ROSES REMEMBERED
Continued from page 68.

Rnd 10: Slip st in first ch-3 sp, work (beginning Cluster, ch 3, Cluster) in same sp, ch 5, work Picot, ch 2, skip next ch-2 sp, sc in next ch-2 sp, 5 dc in next ch-7 sp, skip next ch-2 sp, sc in next ch-2 sp, ch 5, work Picot, ch 2, ★ skip next ch-2 sp, work (Cluster, ch 3, Cluster) in next ch-3 sp, ch 5, work Picot, ch 2, skip next ch-2 sp, sc in next ch-2 sp, 5 dc in next ch-7 sp, skip next ch-2 sp, sc in next ch-2 sp, ch 5, work Picot, ch 2; repeat from ★ around; join with slip st to top of beginning Cluster.

Rnd 11: Ch 1, sc in same st, (sc, ch 3, sc) in next ch-3 sp, sc in next Cluster and in next ch, ch 5, 2 sc in center dc of next 5-dc group, ch 5, skip next Picot and next ch, sc in next ch, ★ sc in next Cluster, (sc, ch 3, sc) in next ch-3 sp, sc in next Cluster and in next ch, ch 5, 2 sc in center dc of next 5-dc group, ch 5, skip next Picot and next ch, sc in next ch; repeat from ★ around; join with slip st to first sc, finish off.

ASSEMBLY

Using Placement Diagram as a guide, join Squares together forming 6 vertical strips of 8 Squares each as follows:

With **right** sides together and working in inside loops only, join yarn with slip st in center ch of first corner; slip st in each st across to center ch of next corner, slip st in center ch; finish off. Join Strips in same manner.

EDGING

Rnd 1: With **right** side facing, join yarn with slip st in any corner ch-3 sp; work (beginning Cluster, ch 3, Cluster) in same sp, ch 2, ★ skip next 2 sc, work Cluster in next sc, ch 2, (skip next 2 sts, work Cluster in next st, ch 2) 5 times, [skip next joining, work Cluster in next ch, ch 2, (skip next 2 sts, work Cluster in next st, ch 2) 6 times] across to next corner ch-3 sp, work (Cluster, ch 3, Cluster) in corner sp, ch 2; repeat from ★ 2 times **more**, skip next 2 sc, work Cluster in next sc, ch 2, (skip next 2 sts, work Cluster in next st, ch 2) 5 times, [skip next joining, work Cluster in next ch, ch 2, (skip next 2 sts, work Cluster in next st, ch 2) 6 times] across; join with slip st to top of beginning Cluster.

Rnd 2: Slip st in next ch-3 sp, ch 1, sc in same sp, ch 5, work Picot, ch 2, (sc in next sp, ch 5, work Picot, ch 2) around; join with slip st to first sc, finish off.

PLACEMENT DIAGRAM

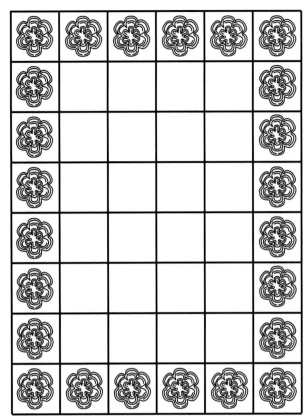

CAREFREE COVER-UP

Wrap yourself in the lush colors of a summer landscape with this carefree throw. The rows of leafy cluster stitches, worked with three shades of green worsted weight yarn, are complemented by lavish fringe.

Finished Size: 51" x 70"

MATERIALS

Worsted Weight Yarn:
   Dk Green - 22 ounces,
      (620 grams, 1,445 yards)
   Green - 13 ounces,
      (370 grams, 855 yards)
   Lt Green - 14 ounces,
      (400 grams, 920 yards)
Crochet hook, size J (6.00 mm) **or** size
   needed for gauge

GAUGE: Sc, (ch 2, Cluster, ch 2, sc) twice
      and 6 rows = 4"

COLOR SEQUENCE

One row **each**: ★ Lt Green, Dk Green, Lt Green, Green, Dk Green, Green; repeat from ★ throughout.

With Lt Green, ch 172 **loosely**.

Row 1 (Wrong side): 2 Dc in fourth ch from hook, skip next 2 chs, sc in next ch, ★ skip next 2 chs, 5 dc in next ch, skip next 2 chs, sc in next ch; repeat from ★ across to last 3 chs, skip next 2 chs, 3 dc in last ch; finish off: 27 5-dc groups.

Note #1: Loop a short piece of yarn around the **back** of any stitch to mark **right** side.

Note #2: To work **Cluster** (uses next 5 sts), ★ YO, insert hook in **next** st, YO and pull up a loop, YO and draw through 2 loops on hook; repeat from ★ 4 times **more**, YO and draw through all 6 loops on hook *(Figs. 9c & d, page 137)*.

Row 2: With **right** side facing, join next color with slip st in first dc; ch 1, sc in same st, ★ ch 2, work Cluster, ch 2, sc in next st; repeat from ★ across; finish off: 28 Clusters.

Row 3: With **wrong** side facing, join next color with slip st in first sc; ch 3 **(counts as first dc, now and throughout)**, 2 dc in same st, sc in next Cluster, ★ 5 dc in next sc, sc in next Cluster; repeat from ★ across to last sc, 3 dc in last sc; finish off: 27 5-dc groups.

Rows 4-102: Repeat Rows 2 and 3, 49 times, then repeat Row 2 once **more**.

EDGING

Rnd 1: With **right** side facing, join Dk Green with slip st in any st; ch 1, sc evenly around, working 3 sc in each corner; join with slip st to first sc.

Rnd 2: Ch 3, do **not** turn; dc in next sc and in each sc around, working 3 dc in center sc of each corner; join with slip st to first dc, finish off.

Holding six strands of Dk Green together, add fringe evenly across short edges of Afghan *(Figs. 29a & c, page 142)*.

SUMMER SHELLS

*Its soft, sandy hue makes our summery afghan a breezy accent
for a vacation cottage. Created with easy double crochets and chain
spaces, the simple shell-over-shell pattern works up quickly.*

Finished Size: 48" x 64"

MATERIALS
Worsted Weight Yarn:
40 ounces, (1,140 grams, 2,745 yards)
Crochet hook, size K (6.50 mm) **or** size
needed for gauge

GAUGE: In pattern, (sc, 5 dc) twice = 3½"
and 8 rows = 4"

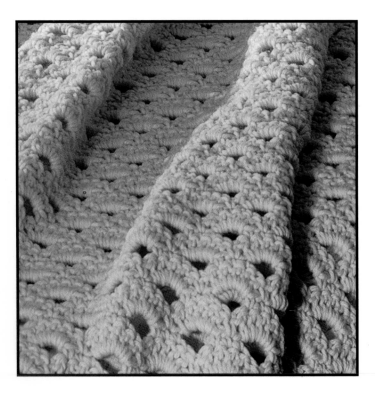

Ch 137 **loosely**.

Row 1 (Right side)**:** Sc in second ch from hook and in next ch,
ch 3, (skip next 2 chs, sc in next 3 chs, ch 3) across to last
4 chs, skip next 2 chs, sc in last 2 chs: 27 ch-3 sps.

Row 2: Ch 1, turn; sc in first sc, (skip next sc, 5 dc in next
ch-3 sp, skip next sc, sc in next sc) across: 27 5-dc groups.

Row 3: Ch 4, turn; skip next dc, sc in next 3 dc, (ch 3, skip
next 3 sts, sc in next 3 dc) across to last 2 sts, ch 1, skip next
dc, hdc in last sc: 26 ch-3 sps.

Row 4: Ch 3, turn; 2 dc in next ch-1 sp, skip next sc, sc in next
sc, (skip next sc, 5 dc in next ch-3 sp, skip next sc, sc in next
sc) across to last sc, skip last sc, 3 dc in last sp: 26 5-dc groups.

Row 5: Ch 1, turn; sc in first 2 dc, ch 3, (skip next 3 sts, sc in
next 3 dc, ch 3) across to last 5 sts, skip next 3 sts, sc in last
2 sts: 27 ch-3 sps.

Repeat Rows 2-5 until Afghan measures 63" from beginning ch,
ending by working Row 3, do **not** finish off.

Edging: Ch 1, sc evenly spaced across end of rows; working in
free loops of beginning ch **(Fig. 23b, page 140)**, 3 sc in first
ch, sc in each ch across to last ch, 3 sc in last ch; sc evenly
spaced across end of rows; sc in each st across working 2 sc in
each ch-3 sp; join with slip st to first sc, finish off.

Using one strand of yarn, add fringe evenly across short edges of
Afghan **(Figs. 29a & c, page 142)**.

2. – Ch 1, turn: sc in first sc, (ship next sc, 5 dc in the next ch-3 sp, ship next sc, sc in the next sc) across.

3. Ch 4, turn: ship next dc, sc in next 3 dc, (ch-3 ship next 3 sts, sc in the 3 dc.) across to last 2 sts, ch-1 ship next dc, hdc in last sc:

4. Ch-3 turn: 2 dc in next ch-1 sp, ship next sc, sc in next sc, (ship next sc, 5 dc in next ch-3 sp, ship next sc, sc in next sc) across to last sc, ship last sc, 3 dc in last sp.

5. Ch-1 turn: sc in first 2 dc, ch-3 (ship next 3 sts, sc in next 3 dc, ch-3) across to last 5 sts ship next 3 sts, sc in last 2 sts.

Summer Shells

Page 78

A Special Note —

OCEAN BREEZE

As soothing as an ocean breeze, this wrap's loose-weave design is created with alternating rows of shell and picot stitches. The afghan works up especially fast because it's crocheted holding two strands of yarn together.

Finished Size: 47" x 60"

MATERIALS
Worsted Weight Yarn:
    57 ounces, (1,620 grams, 3,910 yards)
Crochet hook, size P (10.00 mm) **or** size needed
    for gauge

Note: Entire Afghan is worked holding two strands of yarn
    together.

GAUGE: (Shell, ch 1, Shell) and 5 rows = 4½"

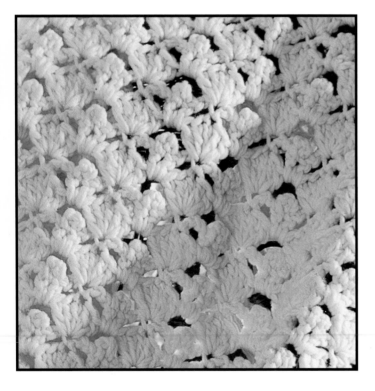

Note: To work **Shell,** 5 dc in st indicated.

Holding two strands of yarn together, ch 112 **loosely**.
Row 1 (Right side)**:** 2 Dc in fourth ch from hook (**3 skipped chs count as first dc**), ch 1, ★ skip next 5 chs, work Shell in next ch, ch 1; repeat from ★ across to last 6 chs, skip next 5 chs, 3 dc in last ch: 17 Shells.
Note #1: Loop a short piece of yarn around any stitch to mark last row as **right** side.
Note #2: To work **Picot,** ch 3, slip st in top of dc just worked.
Row 2: Ch 1, turn; sc in first dc, ★ ch 2, (dc, work Picot, dc) in next ch-1 sp, ch 2, skip next 2 dc, sc in next dc; repeat from ★ across: 18 Picots.
Row 3: Ch 3 (**counts as first dc, now and throughout**), turn; 2 dc in first sc, ch 1, ★ work Shell in next sc, ch 1; repeat from ★ across to last sc, 3 dc in last sc: 17 Shells.
Repeat Rows 2 and 3 until Afghan measures 59" from beginning ch, ending by working Row 3.
Last Row: Ch 1, turn; sc in first dc, ★ ch 2, dc in next ch-1 sp, ch 2, skip next 2 dc, sc in next dc; repeat from ★ across; do **not** finish off.

EDGING
Rnd 1: Ch 1, turn; sc evenly around working 3 sc in each corner; join with slip st to first sc.
Rnd 2: Ch 1, do **not** turn; sc in each sc around working 3 sc in center sc of each corner; join with slip st to first sc, finish off.

Holding four strands of yarn together, add fringe evenly across short edges of Afghan (***Figs. 29a & c, page 142***).

Ocean Breeze

5 7 ounces = 8
(8 oz)

hook -p

Certificate of Quality Assurance

24K or 24KT · 24 Karat Gold

18K or 18KT · 18 Karat Gold

14K or 14KT · 14 Karat Gold

10K or 10KT · 10 Karat Gold

Sterling or 925 · Sterling Silver

Plat. · Platinum

Each piece of jewelry presented on QVC is subject to strict standards of quality and workmanship established by our Quality Assurance Department. Through a systematic inspection program, the Quality Assurance Laboratory ensures that all the jewelry meets or exceeds those rigorous standards. The U.S. Government requires that all karat gold, sterling silver and platinum jewelry have a hallmark that accurately represents precious metal content. To ensure that hallmarks are accurate and comply with U.S. Government requirements, we assay samples of all karat gold, sterling silver and platinum jewelry sold by QVC.

Eric Christopher

Eric Christopher, Vice President, Quality Assurance

QVC QUALITY ASSURANCE LABORATORY

product specification · evaluation · testing · quality

AMERICA

The broad stripes of this patriotic pleaser will be gallantly streaming to commemorate Independence Day. The ripples of red, blue, and off-white are created by working double crochets into the previous row.

Finished Size: 50" x 72"

MATERIALS
Worsted Weight Yarn:
    Off-White - 43 ounces, (1,220 grams, 2,950 yards)
    Red - 11 ounces, (310 grams, 755 yards)
    Blue - 11 ounces, (310 grams, 755 yards)
Crochet hook, size I (5.50 mm) **or** size needed
    for gauge

GAUGE: 14 sts and 15 rows = 4"

COLOR SEQUENCE
2 Rows **each**: Off-White, Red, Off-White, Blue, Off-White, Red;
★ 8 rows Off-White; 2 rows **each**: Blue, Off-White, Red,
Off-White, Blue; 8 rows Off-White; 2 rows **each**: Red,
Off-White, Blue, Off-White, Red; repeat from ★ 6 times **more**,
then 1 row Off-White.

With Off-White, ch 176 **loosely**.
Row 1 (Right side)**:** Sc in second ch from hook and in each ch
across: 175 sc.
Note: Loop a short piece of yarn around any stitch to mark last
row as **right** side.
Row 2: Ch 1, turn; sc in first sc, (ch 1, skip next sc, sc in next
sc) across; finish off.
Row 3: With **right** side facing, join next color with sc in first sc
(see Joining With Sc, page 140); working in **front** of next
ch-1, dc in sc one row **below** ch-1, sc in next sc, ★ working
behind next ch-1, dc in sc one row **below** ch-1, sc in next sc,
working in **front** of next ch-1, dc in sc one row **below** ch-1, sc
in next sc; repeat from ★ across.
Row 4: Ch 1, turn; sc in first sc, (ch 1, skip next dc, sc in next
sc) across; finish off.
Row 5: With **right** side facing, join next color with sc in first sc;
working in **front** of next ch-1, dc in dc one row **below** ch-1, sc
in next sc, ★ working **behind** next ch-1, dc in dc one row
below ch-1, sc in next sc, working in **front** of next ch-1, dc in
dc one row **below** ch-1, sc in next sc; repeat from ★ across.

Row 6: Ch 1, turn; sc in first sc, (ch 1, skip next dc, sc in next
sc) across; finish off.
Rows 7-12: Repeat Rows 5 and 6, 3 times.
Row 13: With **right** side facing, join Off-White with sc in first
sc; working in **front** of next ch-1, dc in dc one row **below** ch-1,
sc in next sc, ★ working **behind** next ch-1, dc in dc one row
below ch-1, sc in next sc, working in **front** of next ch-1, dc in
dc one row **below** ch-1, sc in next sc; repeat from ★ across.
Row 14: Ch 1, turn; sc in first sc, (ch 1, skip next dc, sc in next
sc) across.
Row 15: Ch 1, turn; sc in first sc, working in **front** of next
ch-1, dc in dc one row **below** ch-1, sc in next sc, ★ working
behind next ch-1, dc in dc one row **below** ch-1, sc in next sc,
working in **front** of next ch-1, dc in dc one row **below** ch-1, sc
in next sc; repeat from ★ across.
Row 16: Ch 1, turn; sc in first sc, (ch 1, skip next dc, sc in next
sc) across.
Rows 17-20: Repeat Rows 15 and 16 twice.
Finish off.
Rows 21-30: Repeat Rows 5 and 6, 5 times.
Rows 31-265: Repeat Rows 13-30, 13 times; then repeat
Row 13 once **more**.
Do **not** finish off.

EDGING
TOP
Row 1: Ch 1, turn; sc in first sc, (ch 1, skip next dc, sc in next
sc) across.
Row 2: Ch 1, turn; slip st in first sc and in next ch-1 sp, (ch 1,
slip st in next ch-1 sp) across to last sc, slip st in last sc;
finish off.
BOTTOM
Row 1: With **wrong** side facing and working in free loops of
beginning ch *(Fig. 23b, page 140)*, join Off-White with sc in
first ch; (ch 1, skip next ch, sc in next ch) across.
Row 2: Ch 1, turn; slip st in first sc and in next ch-1 sp, (ch 1,
slip st in next ch-1 sp) across to last sc, slip st in last sc;
finish off.

BROWN-EYED SUSANS

Resembling a meadow of sunny blossoms, this afghan offers a welcome summertime respite. Each brown-eyed Susan block is created with easy cluster stitches and bordered with rich green and gold rounds.

Finished Size: 45" x 59"

MATERIALS
Worsted Weight Yarn:
    Gold - 16 ounces,
       (450 grams, 1,100 yards)
    Brown - 1¹/₂ ounces,
       (40 grams, 105 yards)
    Green - 24 ounces,
       (680 grams, 1,645 yards)
Crochet hook, size G (4.00 mm) **or** size
    needed for gauge
Yarn needle

GAUGE: Each Square = 7"

SQUARE (Make 48)

With Brown, ch 3; join with slip st to form a ring.

Rnd 1 (Right side)**:** Ch 1, 8 sc in ring; join with slip st to first sc.

Note: Loop a short piece of yarn around any stitch to mark last round as **right** side.

Rnd 2: Ch 1, 2 sc in same st and in each sc around; join with slip st to Back Loop Only of first sc *(Fig. 22, page 140)*, finish off: 16 sc.

Note #1: To work **beginning Cluster**, ch 4, ★ YO 3 times, insert hook in st indicated, YO and pull up a loop, (YO and draw through 2 loops on hook) 3 times; repeat from ★ once **more**, YO and draw through all 3 loops on hook *(Figs. 9a & b, page 137)*.

Note #2: To work **Cluster**, ★ YO 3 times, insert hook in sc indicated, YO and pull up a loop, (YO and draw through 2 loops on hook) 3 times; repeat from ★ 2 times **more**, YO and draw through all 4 loops on hook.

Rnd 3: With **right** side facing and working in Back Loops Only, join Gold with slip st in any sc; work beginning Cluster in same st, (ch 1, work Cluster in next sc) 3 times, ch 5, ★ work Cluster in next sc, (ch 1, work Cluster in next sc) 3 times, ch 5; repeat from ★ around; join with slip st to top of beginning Cluster, finish off: 4 loops and 12 ch-1 sps.

Rnd 4: With **right** side facing, join Green with slip st in any loop; ch 3 **(counts as first dc, now and throughout)**, (2 dc, ch 1, 3 dc) in same loop, 3 dc in each ch-1 sp across to next loop, ★ (3 dc, ch 1, 3 dc) in loop, 3 dc in each ch-1 sp across to next loop; repeat from ★ around; join with slip st to first dc, finish off: 60 dc.

Continued on page 93.

WAVES OF GRAIN

A progression of stitch sizes re-creates the rolling waves of wheat and bright summer skies of America's heartland. This radiant afghan is worked with single, half double, double, and treble stitches.

Finished Size: 52" x 70"

MATERIALS

Worsted Weight Yarn:

Gold - 15 ounces, (430 grams, 1,030 yards)
Lt Gold - 11 ounces, (310 grams, 725 yards)
Blue - 13 ounces, (370 grams, 855 yards)
Lt Blue - 8 ounces, (230 grams, 525 yards)
Crochet hook, size I (5.50 mm) **or** size needed for gauge

GAUGE: In pattern, one repeat and 17 rows = 6½"

With Gold, ch 210 **loosely**.

Row 1 (Right side)**:** Sc in second ch from hook, (ch 1, skip next ch, sc in next ch) 3 times, ★ † ch 1, skip next ch, hdc in next ch, ch 1, skip next ch, dc in next ch, ch 1, skip next ch, (tr, ch 1) twice in next ch, tr in next ch, ch 1, (tr, ch 1) twice in next ch, skip next ch, dc in next ch, ch 1, skip next ch, hdc in next ch †, (ch 1, skip next ch, sc in next ch) 7 times; repeat from ★ 6 times **more**, then repeat from † to † once, (ch 1, skip next ch, sc in next ch) 4 times; finish off: 129 sts and 128 ch-1 sps.

Note: Loop a short piece of yarn around any stitch to mark last row as **right** side.

Row 2: With **wrong** side facing, join Lt Gold with sc in first sc *(see Joining With Sc, page 140)*; ★ ch 1, skip next ch, sc in next st; repeat from ★ across; finish off.

Row 3: With **right** side facing, join Blue with slip st in first sc; ch 4 **(counts as first tr, now and throughout)**, tr in next 2 sc, ★ † ch 1, dc in next sc, ch 1, hdc in next sc, ch 1, (sc in next sc, ch 1) 7 times, hdc in next sc, ch 1, dc in next sc, ch 1 †, tr in next 5 sc; repeat from ★ 6 times **more**, then repeat from † to † once, tr in last 3 sc; finish off: 129 sts and 96 ch-1 sps.

Row 4: With **wrong** side facing, join Lt Blue with sc in first tr; ch 1, skip next tr, sc in next tr, ch 1, (skip next ch, sc in next st, ch 1) 12 times, ★ (skip next tr, sc in next tr, ch 1) twice, (skip next ch, sc in next st, ch 1) 12 times; repeat from ★ across to last 2 tr, skip next tr, sc in last tr; finish off.

Row 5: With **right** side facing, join Gold with sc in first sc; (ch 1, sc in next sc) 3 times, ★ † ch 1, hdc in next sc, ch 1, dc in next sc, ch 1, tr in next sc, (ch 1, tr in next ch-1 sp, ch 1, tr in next sc) twice, ch 1, dc in next sc, ch 1, hdc in next sc †, (ch 1, sc in next sc) 7 times; repeat from ★ 6 times **more**, then repeat from † to † once, (ch 1, sc in next sc) 4 times; finish off: 129 sts and 128 ch-1 sps.

Row 6: With **wrong** side facing, join Lt Gold with sc in first sc; ★ ch 1, skip next ch, sc in next st; repeat from ★ across; finish off.

Repeat Rows 3-6 until Afghan measures 70" from beginning ch, ending by working Row 6; do **not** finish off.

EDGING

Top: Ch 1, turn; slip st in first sc and in next ch-1 sp, (ch 1, slip st in next ch-1 sp) across to last sc, slip st in last sc; finish off.

Bottom: With **right** side facing, join Gold with slip st in free loop of first ch *(Fig. 23b, page 140)*; (slip st in next ch-1 sp, ch 1) 6 times, skip next ch, slip st in free loop of next ch, ch 1, ★ (slip st in next ch-1 sp, ch 1) 12 times, skip next ch, slip st in free loop of next ch, ch 1; repeat from ★ 6 times **more**, (slip st in next ch-1 sp, ch 1) 5 times, slip st in next ch-1 sp and in free loop of next ch; finish off.

VICTORIAN SUMMER

The thriving green lawns of summer inspired this Victorian-look throw. Rows of elegant shell stitches create the center portion of the afghan, and the lacy edging features a fancy pineapple design.

Finished Size: 50" x 72"

MATERIALS

Worsted Weight Yarn:
50 ounces, (1,420 grams, 3,150 yards)
Crochet hook, size H (5.00 mm) **or** size needed for gauge

GAUGE: 4 Shells and 7 rows = 4"

Note: To work **Shell**, (2 dc, ch 2, 2 dc) in st or sp indicated.

Ch 224 **loosely**.

Row 1: Work Shell in sixth ch from hook, ★ skip next 4 chs, work Shell in next ch; repeat from ★ across to last 3 chs, skip next 2 chs, dc in last ch: 44 Shells.

Row 2 (Right side)**:** Ch 3 **(counts as first dc, now and throughout)**, turn; work Shell in each Shell (ch-2 sp) across, dc in top of beginning ch.

Note: Loop a short piece of yarn around any stitch to mark last row as **right** side.

Row 3: Ch 3, turn; work Shell in each Shell across, dc in last dc.

Repeat Row 3 until Afghan measures 66" from beginning ch, ending by working a **wrong** side row; do **not** finish off.

EDGING

Rnd 1: Ch 1, turn; 3 sc in corner, work 173 sc evenly spaced across to next corner, 3 sc in corner; work 269 sc evenly spaced across end of rows to next corner, 3 sc in corner; working over beginning ch, work 173 sc evenly spaced across to next corner, 3 sc in corner; work 269 sc evenly spaced across end of rows; join with slip st to first sc: 896 sc.

Note: To work **V-St**, (dc, ch 3, dc) in sc indicated.

Rnd 2: Slip st in next sc, ch 3, dc in same st, † ch 3, skip next 3 sc, work V-St in next sc, (ch 3, skip next 5 sc, 2 dc in next sc, ch 3, skip next 5 sc, work V-St in next sc) 14 times, ch 3, skip next 3 sc, 2 dc in corner sc, ch 3, skip next 3 sc, work V-St in next sc, (ch 3, skip next 5 sc, 2 dc in next sc, ch 3, skip next 5 sc, work V-St in next sc) 22 times, ch 3, skip next 3 sc †, 2 dc in corner sc, repeat from † to † once; join with slip st to first dc.

Rnd 3: Ch 3, dc in next dc, ch 2, skip next ch-3 sp, 9 dc in next ch-3 sp, ch 2, ★ dc in next 2 dc, ch 2, skip next ch-3 sp, 9 dc in next ch-3 sp, ch 2; repeat from ★ around; join with slip st to first dc.

Rnd 4: Ch 3, dc in same st, ch 2, 2 dc in next dc, ch 2, † sc in next dc, (ch 3, skip next dc, sc in next dc) 4 times, ch 2, [dc in next 2 dc, ch 2, sc in next dc, (ch 3, skip next dc, sc in next dc) 4 times, ch 2] 14 times, (2 dc in next dc, ch 2) twice, sc in next dc, (ch 3, skip next dc, sc in next dc) 4 times, ch 2, [dc in next 2 dc, ch 2, sc in next dc, (ch 3, skip next dc, sc in next dc) 4 times, ch 2] 22 times †, (2 dc in next dc, ch 2) twice, repeat from † to † once; join with slip st to first dc.

Rnd 5: Ch 3, dc in next dc, † ch 2, 2 dc in next ch-2 sp, ch 2, dc in next 2 dc, ch 2, skip next ch-2 sp, sc in next ch-3 sp, (ch 3, sc in next ch-3 sp) 3 times, ch 2, [dc in next 2 dc, ch 2, skip next ch-2 sp, sc in next ch-3 sp, (ch 3, sc in next ch-3 sp) 3 times, ch 2] 14 times, dc in next 2 dc, ch 2, 2 dc in next ch-2 sp, ch 2, dc in next 2 dc, ch 2, skip next ch-2 sp, sc in next ch-3 sp, (ch 3, sc in next ch-3 sp) 3 times, ch 2, [dc in next 2 dc, ch 2, skip next ch-2 sp, sc in next ch-3 sp, (ch 3, sc in next ch-3 sp) 3 times, ch 2] 22 times †, dc in next 2 dc, repeat from † to † once; join with slip st to first dc.

Continued on page 93.

COUNTRY LANE

Travel down any country lane and discover the delightful spectrum of roadside wildflowers reflected in this granny square afghan. Our convenient placement diagram makes it easy to whipstitch the floral motifs together.

Finished Size: 55" x 58"

MATERIALS

Worsted Weight Yarn:

Green - 27 ounces, (770 grams, 1,850 yards)

Lt Green - 28 ounces, (800 grams, 1,920 yards)

Lt Pink - ½ ounce, (20 grams, 35 yards)

Pink - 1 ounce, (30 grams, 70 yards)

Dk Pink - 1 ounce, (30 grams, 70 yards)

Rose - 1½ ounces, (40 grams, 105 yards)

Lt Blue - 2 ounces, (60 grams, 140 yards)

Blue - 2½ ounces, (70 grams, 170 yards)

Lt Purple - 3 ounces, (90 grams, 205 yards)

Purple - 3 ounces, (90 grams, 205 yards)

Dk Purple - 3½ ounces, (100 grams, 240 yards)

Crochet hook, size G (4.00 mm) **or** size needed for gauge

Yarn needle

GAUGE: Each Square = 2¼"

SOLID SQUARE (Make 306)

With Green, ch 5; join with slip st to form a ring.

Rnd 1 (Right side)**:** Ch 3 **(counts as first dc, now and throughout)**, 2 dc in ring, ch 3, (3 dc in ring, ch 3) 3 times; join with slip st to first dc: 4 ch-3 sps.

Note: Loop a short piece of yarn around any stitch to mark last round as **right** side.

Rnd 2: Slip st in next 2 dc and in next ch-3 sp, ch 3, (2 dc, ch 3, 3 dc) in same sp, ch 1, ★ (3 dc, ch 3, 3 dc) in next ch-3 sp, ch 1; repeat from ★ around; join with slip st to first dc, finish off: 24 dc.

FLOWER SQUARE (Make 342)

For Rnd 1, make the number of Squares indicated with the following colors: Lt Pink - 6, Pink - 14, Dk Pink - 22, Rose - 30, Lt Blue - 38, Blue - 46, Lt Purple - 54, Purple - 62, Dk Purple - 70.

Ch 5; join with slip st to form a ring.

Rnd 1 (Right side)**:** Ch 3, 2 dc in ring, ch 3, (3 dc in ring, ch 3) 3 times; join with slip st to first dc, finish off: 4 ch-3 sps.

Note: Mark last round as **right** side.

Rnd 2: With **right** side facing, join Lt Green with slip st in any ch-3 sp; ch 3, (2 dc, ch 3, 3 dc) in same sp, ch 1, ★ (3 dc, ch 3, 3 dc) in next ch-3 sp, ch 1; repeat from ★ around; join with slip st to first dc, finish off: 24 dc.

ASSEMBLY

With Lt Green and using Placement Diagram as a guide, page 92, whipstitch Squares together forming diagonal strips *(Fig. 28b, page 142)*, beginning in center ch of first corner and ending in center ch of next corner; then whipstitch strips together in same manner.

EDGING

With **right** side facing, join Lt Green with slip st in any dc; ch 1, sc evenly around working 3 sc in each corner ch-3 sp; join with slip st to first sc, finish off.

PLACEMENT DIAGRAM

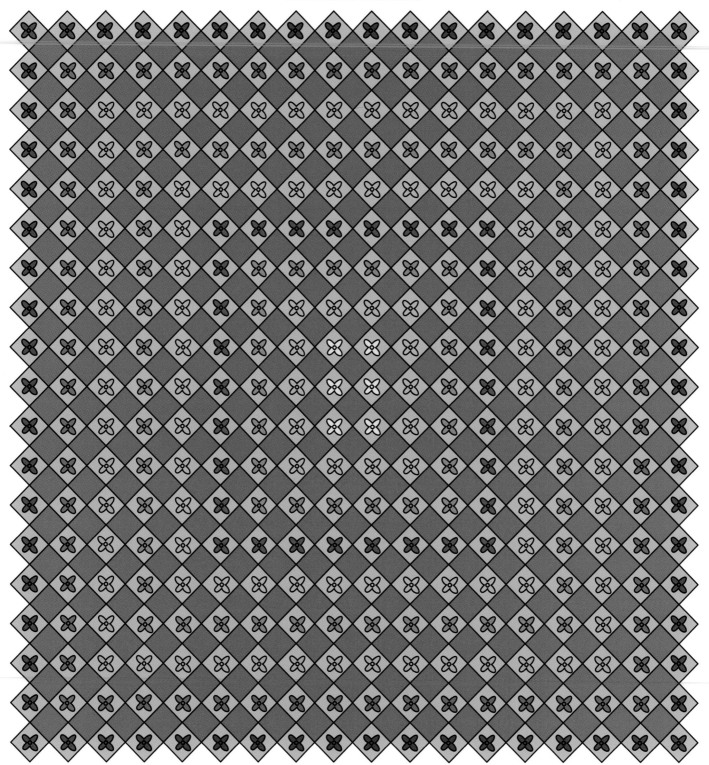

BROWN-EYED SUSANS Continued from page 84.

Rnd 5: With **right** side facing and working in both loops, join Gold with slip st in any ch-1 sp; ch 3, (dc, ch 3, 2 dc) in same sp, dc in each dc across to next ch-1 sp, ★ (2 dc, ch 3, 2 dc) in ch-1 sp, dc in each dc across to next ch-1 sp; repeat from ★ around; join with slip st to first dc, finish off: 76 dc.

Rnd 6: With **right** side facing, join Green with slip st in any ch-3 sp; ch 3, (dc, ch 3, 2 dc) in same sp, dc in each dc across to next ch-3 sp, ★ (2 dc, ch 3, 2 dc) in ch-3 sp, dc in each dc across to next ch-3 sp; repeat from ★ around; join with slip st to first dc, do **not** finish off: 92 dc.

Rnd 7: Ch 1, sc in same st and in next dc, (sc, ch 2, sc) in next ch-3 sp, ★ sc in each dc across to next ch-3 sp, (sc, ch 2, sc) in ch-3 sp; repeat from ★ 2 times **more**, sc in each dc across; join with slip st to first sc, finish off: 100 sc.

ASSEMBLY

With Green, whipstitch Squares together forming 6 vertical strips of 8 Squares each **(Fig. 28b, page 142)**, beginning in second ch of first corner ch-2 and ending in first ch of next corner ch-2; then whipstitch strips together in same manner.

EDGING

Rnd 1: With **right** side facing, join Green with slip st in any sc; ch 3, dc evenly around working (2 dc, ch 3, 2 dc) in each corner ch-2 sp; join with slip st to first dc.

Rnd 2: Ch 3, dc in next dc and in each dc around working (2 dc, ch 3, 2 dc) in each corner ch-3 sp; join with slip st to first dc, finish off.

VICTORIAN SUMMER Continued from page 88.

Rnd 6: Ch 6 **(counts as first dc plus ch 3, now and throughout)**, † (dc in next 2 dc, ch 3) twice, dc in next dc, ch 2, skip next ch-2 sp, sc in next ch-3 sp, (ch 3, sc in next ch-3 sp) twice, ch 2, [dc in next dc, ch 3, dc in next dc, ch 2, skip next ch-2 sp, sc in next ch-3 sp, (ch 3, sc in next ch-3 sp) twice, ch 2] 14 times, dc in next dc, ch 3, (dc in next 2 dc, ch 3) twice, dc in next dc, ch 2, skip next ch-2 sp, sc in next ch-3 sp, (ch 3, sc in next ch-3 sp) twice, ch 2, [dc in next dc, ch 3, dc in next dc, ch 2, skip next ch-2 sp, sc in next ch-3 sp, (ch 3, sc in next ch-3 sp) twice, ch 2] 22 times †, dc in next dc, ch 3, repeat from † to † once; join with slip st to first dc.

Rnd 7: Slip st in first ch-3 sp, ch 6, sc in third ch from hook, dc in same sp, (ch 3, sc in dc just made, dc in same sp) 3 times, ch 2, sc in next ch-3 sp, ch 2, † dc in next ch-3 sp, (ch 3, sc in dc just made, dc in same sp) 4 times, ch 2, skip next ch-2 sp, sc in next ch-3 sp, ch 3, sc in next ch-3 sp, ch 2 †, repeat from † to † 14 times **more**, dc in next ch-3 sp, (ch 3, sc in dc just made, dc in same sp) 4 times, ch 2, sc in next ch-3 sp, ch 2, repeat from † to † 23 times, dc in next ch-3 sp, (ch 3, sc in dc just made, dc in same sp) 4 times, ch 2, sc in next ch-3 sp, ch 2, repeat from † to † 15 times, dc in next ch-3 sp, (ch 3, sc in dc in just made, dc in same sp) 4 times, ch 2, sc in next ch-3 sp, ch 2, repeat from † to † 23 times; join with slip st to third ch of beginning ch-6, finish off.

GOLDEN RULE

A "classy" gift for a teacher, this throw is punctuated with gently curving stripes. Double crochets and chains are worked behind the decorative picots to multiply the lovely texture.

Finished Size: 52" x 71"

MATERIALS

Worsted Weight Yarn:
  Green - 20 ounces,
    (570 grams, 1,260 yards)
  Maroon - 19 ounces,
    (540 grams, 1,135 yards)
  Gold - 19 ounces,
    (540 grams, 1,135 yards)
Crochet hook, size I (5.50 mm) **or** size
  needed for gauge

GAUGE: One repeat (point to point) = 4¼"
    and 9 rows = 4"

COLOR SEQUENCE
2 Rows **each**: ★ Green, Maroon, Gold; repeat from ★ throughout, ending by working 3 rows of Green.

Note: To **decrease** (uses next 3 sts), YO, insert hook in next ch or st, YO and pull up a loop, YO and draw through 2 loops on hook, skip next ch or st, YO, insert hook in next ch or st, YO and pull up a loop, YO and draw through 2 loops on hook, YO and draw through all 3 loops on hook.

With Green, ch 231 **loosely**.

Row 1 (Right side)**:** Dc in fourth ch from hook, ★ † ch 1, (skip next ch, dc in next ch, ch 1) 3 times, skip next ch, (dc, ch 3, dc) in next ch, ch 1, (skip next ch, dc in next ch, ch 1) 3 times †, skip next ch, YO, insert hook in next ch, YO and pull up a loop, YO and draw through 2 loops on hook, skip next 2 chs, YO, insert hook in next ch, YO and pull up a loop, YO and draw through 2 loops on hook, YO and draw through all 3 loops on hook; repeat from ★ 10 times **more**, then repeat from † to † once, skip next ch, decrease: 108 sps.

Note #1: Loop a short piece of yarn around any stitch to mark last row as **right** side.

Note #2: To work **Picot**, ch 3, dc in third ch from hook.

Row 2: Ch 1, turn; sc in first st, (ch 1, sc in next dc) twice, (work Picot, sc in next dc) 5 times, ch 1, ★ (skip next ch-1 sp, sc in next st) 3 times, ch 1, sc in next dc, (work Picot, sc in next dc) 5 times, ch 1; repeat from ★ across to last 2 dc, sc in next dc, ch 1, sc in last dc; finish off: 60 Picots.

Row 3: With **right** side facing, join next color with slip st in first sc; ch 2, (dc in next sc, ch 1) 4 times, ★ † working **behind** Picot, (dc, ch 3, dc) in ch-3 sp one row **below** next Picot, ch 1, (dc in next sc, ch 1) 3 times, skip next ch-1 sp, decrease †, ch 1, (dc in next sc, ch 1) 3 times; repeat from ★ 10 times **more**, then repeat from † to † once: 108 sps.

Row 4: Ch 1, turn; sc in first st, (ch 1, sc in next dc) twice, (work Picot, sc in next dc) 5 times, ★ ch 1, sc in next dc, ch 3, working **behind** decrease, sc in skipped sc one row **below** next decrease, ch 3, sc in next dc, ch 1, sc in next dc, (work Picot, sc in next dc) 5 times; repeat from ★ 10 times **more**, (ch 1, sc in next dc) twice; finish off: 60 Picots.

Continued on page 104.

RODEO STARS

Worked holding two strands of yarn together, this afghan will be the star of the rodeo because it's finished in record time! The three panels are created with rows of plush star stitches and openwork rows of double crochets. The panels are completed with openwork borders and then whipstitched together.

Finished Size: 48" x 63"

MATERIALS

Worsted Weight Yarn:
46 ounces, (1,310 grams, 3,025 yards)
Crochet hook, size N (9.00 mm) **or** size needed for gauge
Yarn needle

Note: Entire Afghan is worked holding two strands of yarn together.

GAUGE: In pattern, 5 sts = 4" and 8 rows = 6"

STAR PANEL (Make 3)

Holding two strands of yarn together, ch 35 **loosely**.

Row 1: YO, insert hook in third ch from hook, YO and pull up a loop, skip next ch, YO, insert hook in next ch, YO and pull up a loop, YO and draw through all 5 loops on hook, ★ ch 1, YO, insert hook in **same** ch as last loop of last st, YO and pull up a loop, skip next ch, YO, insert hook in next ch, YO and pull up a loop, YO and draw through all 5 loops on hook; repeat from ★ across: 15 ch-1 sps.

Note #1: To work **beginning Star Stitch**, YO, insert hook in first st at base of turning ch, YO and pull up a loop, YO, skip next ch, insert hook in next st *(Fig. 1)*, YO and pull up a loop, YO and draw through all 5 loops on hook, ch 1 to close.

Note #2: To work **Star Stitch**, YO, insert hook in **same** st as last loop of last st, YO and pull up a loop, YO, skip next ch, insert hook in next st, YO and pull up a loop, YO and draw through all 5 loops on hook, ch 1 to close.

Fig. 1

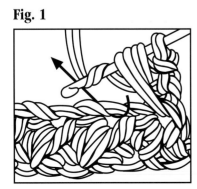

Rows 2-4: Ch 3, turn; work beginning Star St, work Star Sts across to last st, YO, insert hook in **same** st as last loop of last st, YO and pull up a loop, YO, insert hook in top of beginning ch, YO and pull up a loop, YO and draw through all 5 loops on hook.

Row 5: Ch 4 **(counts as first dc plus ch 1, now and throughout)**, turn; (skip next ch, dc in next st, ch 1) across to last st, dc in top of beginning ch-3: 17 dc.

Rows 6-8: Ch 4, turn; dc in next dc, (ch 1, dc in next dc) across.

Row 9: Ch 3, turn; YO, insert hook in first dc, YO and pull up a loop, YO, insert hook in next dc, YO and pull up a loop, YO and draw through all 5 loops on hook, ★ ch 1, YO, insert hook in **same** dc as last loop of last st, YO and pull up a loop, YO, insert hook in next dc, YO and pull up a loop, YO and draw through all 5 loops on hook; repeat from ★ across.

Repeat Rows 2-9 until Panel measures 58" from beginning ch, ending by working Row 4; do **not** finish off.

PANEL EDGING

Rnd 1: Ch 1, turn; 3 sc in same st, working in each st and in each ch-1 sp, work 31 sc evenly spaced across to last st, 3 sc in last st; work 129 sc evenly spaced across end of rows to beginning ch; working in free loops of beginning ch *(Fig. 23b, page 140)*, 3 sc in first ch, sc in each ch across to last ch, 3 sc in last ch; work 129 sc evenly spaced across end of rows; join with slip st to first sc: 332 sc.

Rnd 2 (Right side): Slip st in next sc, ch 4, turn; skip next sc, (dc in next sc, ch 1, skip next sc) across to next corner sc, ★ (dc, ch 1) 3 times in corner sc, skip next sc, (dc in next sc, ch 1, skip next sc) across to next corner; repeat from ★ 2 times **more**, (dc, ch 1) twice in same st as first dc; join with slip st to first dc.

Note: Loop a short piece of yarn around last stitch to mark **right** side and top edge.

Rnd 3: Ch 4, turn; (dc, ch 1) 3 times in corner dc, ★ (dc in next dc, ch 1) across to next corner, (dc, ch 1) 3 times in corner dc; repeat from ★ 2 times **more**, (dc in next dc, ch 1) across; join with slip st to first dc, finish off.

Continued on page 104.

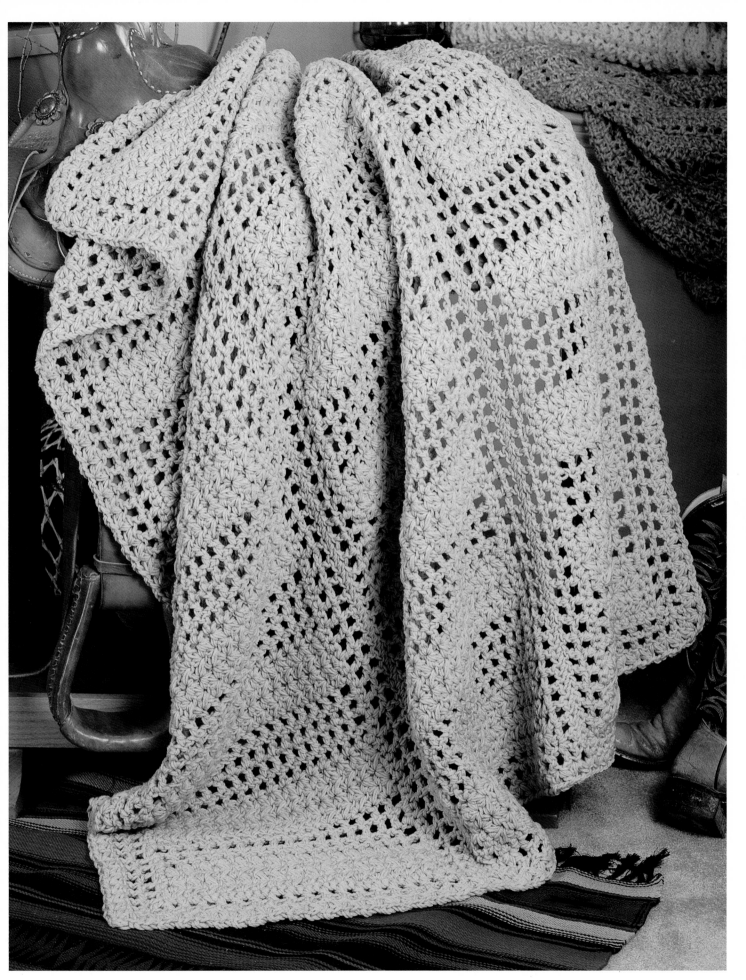

ROSE GARDEN

Create a Grandparents' Day delight with this blossoming "pillowghan" —
it folds into a pocket square to form a clever pillow! The dimensional
rosy flowers on each block are worked as you go using easy chain spaces
and double crochets. Rounds of popcorn stitches accent the motifs.

Finished Size: 47" x 62"

MATERIALS

Worsted Weight Yarn:

Rose - 1½ ounces, (40 grams, 100 yards)
Dk Rose - 5 ounces, (140 grams, 330 yards)
Black - 13 ounces, (370 grams, 855 yards)
Green - 6 ounces, (170 grams, 395 yards)
Dk Green - 7 ounces, (200 grams, 460 yards)
Beige - 2 ounces, (60 grams, 135 yards)
Taupe - 15 ounces, (430 grams, 985 yards)
Crochet hook, size H (5.00 mm) **or** size needed
for gauge

GAUGE: 14 dc = 4"

Each Square = 15½"

SQUARE (Make 13)

With Rose, ch 6; join with slip st to form a ring.

Rnd 1 (Right side)**:** Ch 1, 18 sc in ring; join with slip st to
first sc.

Note: Loop a short piece of yarn around any stitch to mark last
round as **right** side.

Rnd 2: Ch 3, skip next 2 sc, ★ slip st in next sc, ch 3, skip next
2 sc; repeat from ★ around; join with slip st to first slip st:
6 ch-3 sps.

Rnd 3: Slip st in first ch-3 sp, ch 1, (sc, ch 3, 5 dc, ch 3, sc) in
same sp and in each ch-3 sp around; join with slip st to first sc,
finish off: 6 Petals.

Rnd 4: With **right** side facing, join Dk Rose with slip st in first sc
of any Petal; ch 1, sc in same st, ch 5, ★ sc in first sc of next
Petal, ch 5; repeat from ★ around; join with slip st to first sc:
6 loops.

Rnd 5: Slip st in first loop, ch 1, (sc, ch 3, 7 dc, ch 3, sc) in
same loop and in each loop around; join with slip st to first sc,
finish off: 6 Petals.

Rnd 6: With **right** side facing, join Black with slip st in first sc of
any Petal; ch 1, sc in same st, ch 6, ★ sc in first sc of next Petal,
ch 6; repeat from ★ around; join with slip st to first sc: 6 loops.

Rnd 7: Slip st in first loop, ch 3 **(counts as first dc, now and
throughout)**, (4 dc, ch 2, dc) in same loop, † 6 dc in next
loop, (2 dc, ch 2, 4 dc) in next loop †, (5 dc, ch 2, dc) in next
loop, repeat from † to † once; join with slip st to first dc: 36 dc.

Rnd 8: Ch 3, dc in next 4 dc, (3 dc, ch 2, 3 dc) in next ch-2 sp
(corner), ★ dc in each dc across to next ch-2 sp, (3 dc, ch 2,
3 dc) in ch-2 sp; repeat from ★ 2 times **more**, dc in each dc
across; join with slip st to first dc, finish off: 60 dc.

Rnd 9: With **right** side facing, join Green with slip st in any
corner ch-2 sp; ch 3, (2 dc, ch 2, 3 dc) in same sp, ch 1,
(skip next 3 dc, 3 dc in next dc, ch 1) 3 times, skip next 3 dc,
★ (3 dc, ch 2, 3 dc) in next corner ch-2 sp, ch 1, skip next
3 dc, (3 dc in next dc, ch 1, skip next 3 dc) 3 times; repeat
from ★ around; join with slip st to first dc, finish off.

Rnd 10: With **right** side facing, join Dk Green with slip st in
any corner ch-2 sp; ch 3, (2 dc, ch 2, 3 dc) in same sp, ch 1,
(3 dc in next ch-1 sp, ch 1) 4 times, ★ (3 dc, ch 2, 3 dc) in
next corner ch-2 sp, ch 1, (3 dc in next ch-1 sp, ch 1) 4 times;
repeat from ★ around; join with slip st to first dc, finish off:
72 dc.

Rnd 11: With **right** side facing, join Beige with slip st in any
corner ch-2 sp; ch 3, (dc, ch 3, 2 dc) in same sp, dc in each dc
across to next corner ch-2 sp, ★ (2 dc, ch 3, 2 dc) in corner
ch-2 sp, dc in each dc across to next corner ch-2 sp; repeat
from ★ around; join with slip st to first dc, finish off: 88 dc.

Note: To work **Popcorn**, 5 dc in next dc, drop loop from hook,
insert hook in first dc of 5-dc group, hook dropped loop and
draw through *(Fig. 10b, page 137)*.

Rnd 12: With **right** side facing, join Taupe with slip st in any
corner ch-3 sp; ch 3, (dc, ch 3, 2 dc) in same sp, work
Popcorn, (dc in next 2 dc, work Popcorn) across to next corner
ch-3 sp, ★ (2 dc, ch 3, 2 dc) in corner ch-3 sp, work Popcorn,
(dc in next 2 dc, work Popcorn) across to next corner ch-3 sp;
repeat from ★ around; join with slip st to first dc, finish off:
32 Popcorns.

Continued on page 105.

PRIMARILY FOR KIDS

Welcome your little one home from school with this comfy wrap — it's ideal for study time! Worked holding two strands of yarn together, the motifs are made with double crochet clusters and long double crochets. Each square is edged with a simple black border, emphasizing the bold crayon-inspired hues.

Finished Size: 45" x 63"

MATERIALS
Worsted Weight Yarn:
Black - 41 ounces, (1,160 grams, 2,390 yards)
Scraps - 30 ounces, (850 grams, 1,750 yards) **total**
Crochet hook, size N (9.00 mm) **or** size needed
for gauge
Yarn needle

Note: Entire Afghan is worked holding two strands of yarn together.

GAUGE: Each Square = 9"

STITCH GUIDE

3-DC CLUSTER
★ YO, insert hook in sp indicated, YO and pull up a loop, YO and draw through 2 loops on hook; repeat from ★ 2 times **more**, YO and draw through all 4 loops on hook *(Figs. 9a & b, page 137)*.

4-DC CLUSTER
★ YO, insert hook in ch-2 sp indicated, YO and pull up a loop, YO and draw through 2 loops on hook; repeat from ★ 3 times **more**, YO and draw through all 5 loops on hook.

LONG DOUBLE CROCHET *(abbreviated Ldc)*
YO, insert hook in dc one rnd **below** next sp, YO and pull up a loop even with hook *(Fig. 1)*, (YO and draw through 2 loops on hook) twice.

Fig. 1

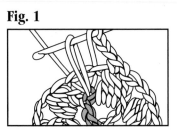

2-DC CLUSTER
★ YO, insert hook in st or sp indicated, YO and pull up a loop, YO and draw through 2 loops on hook; repeat from ★ once **more**, YO and draw through all 3 loops on hook.

SQUARE #1 (Make 9)

With desired color, ch 4; join with slip st to form a ring.
Rnd 1 (Right side): Ch 5, (dc in ring, ch 2) 7 times; join with slip st to third ch of beginning ch-5: 8 ch-2 sps.
Note: Loop a short piece of yarn around any stitch to mark last round as **right** side.
Rnd 2: Slip st in first ch-2 sp, ch 2, work 3-dc Cluster in same sp, ch 3, (work 4-dc Cluster in next ch-2 sp, ch 3) around; skip beginning ch-2 and join with slip st to top of first Cluster, finish off.
Rnd 3: With **right** side facing, join next color with slip st in any Cluster; ch 1, sc in same st, ch 3, work Ldc, ch 3, ★ sc in next Cluster, ch 3, work Ldc, ch 3; repeat from ★ around; join with slip st to first sc: 16 ch-3 sps.
Rnd 4: Slip st in first 2 chs, ch 1, sc in same sp, ch 4, (sc in next ch-3 sp, ch 4) around; join with slip st to first sc.
Rnd 5: Slip st in first 2 chs, ch 1, sc in same sp, ch 3, (sc in next ch-4 sp, ch 3) twice, (2 dc, ch 2, 2 dc) in next ch-4 sp, ch 3, ★ (sc in next ch-4 sp, ch 3) 3 times, (2 dc, ch 2, 2 dc) in next ch-4 sp, ch 3; repeat from ★ around; join with slip st to first sc, finish off.
Rnd 6: With **right** side facing, join Black with slip st in any ch-2 sp; ch 3 **(counts as first dc, now and throughout)**, (dc, ch 2, 2 dc) in same sp, skip next dc, dc in next dc, 2 dc in each of next 2 ch-3 sps, dc in next sc, 2 dc in each of next 2 ch-3 sps, dc in next dc, skip next dc, ★ (2 dc, ch 2, 2 dc) in next ch-2 sp, skip next dc, dc in next dc, 2 dc in each of next 2 ch-3 sps, dc in next sc, 2 dc in each of next 2 ch-3 sps, dc in next dc, skip next dc; repeat from ★ around; join with slip st to first dc: 60 dc.
Rnd 7: Ch 3, dc in next dc, (2 dc, ch 2, 2 dc) in next ch-2 sp, ★ dc in each dc across to next ch-2 sp, (2 dc, ch 2, 2 dc) in ch-2 sp; repeat from ★ 2 times **more**, dc in each dc across; join with slip st to first dc, finish off: 76 dc.

Continued on page 102.

SQUARE #2 (Make 9)

With desired color, ch 4; join with slip st to form a ring.

Rnd 1 (Right side): Ch 4 **(counts as first dc plus ch 1)**, (dc in ring, ch 1) 11 times; join with slip st to first dc, finish off: 12 ch-1 sps.

Note: Mark last round as **right** side.

Rnd 2: With **right** side facing, join next color with slip st in any dc; ch 6, (work 3-dc Cluster in next ch-1 sp, ch 2) 3 times, ★ tr in next dc, ch 2, (work 3-dc Cluster in next ch-1 sp, ch 2) 3 times; repeat from ★ around; join with slip st to fourth ch of beginning ch-6: 12 3-dc Clusters.

Rnd 3: Ch 6, ★ † 5 dc in next ch-2 sp, ch 2, skip next 3-dc Cluster, sc in next 3-dc Cluster, ch 2, skip next ch-2 sp, 5 dc in next ch-2 sp, ch 2 †, tr in next tr, ch 2; repeat from ★ 2 times **more**, then repeat from † to † once; join with slip st to fourth ch of beginning ch-6, finish off.

Rnd 4: With **right** side facing, join Black with slip st in first ch-2 sp; ch 3, dc in same sp, ★ † skip next dc, dc in next 4 dc and in next ch-2 sp, work 2-dc Cluster in next sc, dc in next ch-2 sp and in next 4 dc, skip next dc, 2 dc in next ch-2 sp, ch 2 †, 2 dc in next ch-2 sp; repeat from ★ 2 times **more**, then repeat from † to † once; join with slip st to first dc: 60 sts and 4 ch-2 sps.

Rnd 5: Ch 4 **(counts as first tr, now and throughout)**, ★ tr in next dc and in each st across to next ch-2 sp, (2 tr, ch 2, 2 tr) in ch-2 sp; repeat from ★ around; join with slip st to first tr, finish off: 76 tr.

SQUARE #3 (Make 9)

With desired color, ch 4; join with slip st to form a ring.

Rnd 1 (Right side): Ch 5, (dc in ring, ch 2) 7 times; join with slip st to third ch of beginning ch-5: 8 ch-2 sps.

Note: Mark last round as **right** side.

Rnd 2: Slip st in first ch-2 sp, ch 3, 3 dc in same sp, ch 2, (4 dc in next ch-2 sp, ch 2) around; join with slip st to first dc, finish off: 32 dc.

Rnd 3: With **right** side facing, join next color with slip st in first dc of any 4-dc group; ch 1, sc in same st and in next 3 dc, work Ldc, (sc in next 4 dc, work Ldc) around; join with slip st to first sc, finish off: 40 sts.

Rnd 4: With **right** side facing, join next color with slip st in any Ldc; ch 3, 4 dc in same st, (tr, 2 dc, ch 2, 2 dc, tr) in next Ldc, ★ 5 dc in next Ldc, (tr, 2 dc, ch 2, 2 dc, tr) in next Ldc; repeat from ★ around; join with slip st to first dc, finish off: 44 sts and 4 ch-2 sps.

Rnd 5: With **right** side facing, join Black with slip st in any ch-2 sp; ch 3, (dc, ch 2, 2 dc) in same sp, dc in each st across to next ch-2 sp, ★ (2 dc, ch 2, 2 dc) in ch-2 sp, dc in each st across to next ch-2 sp; repeat from ★ around; join with slip st to first dc: 60 dc.

Rnd 6: Ch 3, dc in next dc, (2 dc, ch 2, 2 dc) in next ch-2 sp, ★ dc in each dc across to next ch-2 sp, (2 dc, ch 2, 2 dc) in ch-2 sp; repeat from ★ 2 times **more**, dc in each dc across; join with slip st to first dc, finish off: 76 dc.

SQUARE #4 (Make 8)

With desired color, ch 4; join with slip st to form a ring.

Rnd 1 (Right side)**:** Ch 1, ★ sc in ring, ch 5, work 2-dc Cluster in ring, ch 5; repeat from ★ 3 times **more**; join with slip st to first sc, finish off: 8 loops.

Note: Mark last round as **right** side.

Rnd 2: With **right** side facing, join next color with slip st in any loop; ch 3, 2 dc in same loop, ch 2, (3 dc in next loop, ch 2) around; join with slip st to first dc, finish off: 24 dc.

Rnd 3: With **right** side facing, join next color with slip st in third dc of any 3-dc group; ch 1, sc in same st, ★ † work 3-dc Cluster in next ch-2 sp, sc in next dc, ch 1, skip next dc, sc in next dc, work 2-dc Cluster in next ch-2 sp, (ch 1, work 2-dc Cluster in same sp) twice, sc in next dc, ch 1, skip next dc †, sc in next dc; repeat from ★ 2 times **more**, then repeat from † to † once; join with slip st to first sc, finish off: 32 sts and 16 ch-1 sps.

Rnd 4: With **right** side facing, join Black with slip st in center 2-dc Cluster of any 3-Cluster group; ch 3, (dc, ch 2, 2 dc) in same st, ★ † dc in next ch-1 sp and in next 2 sts, work Ldc, dc in next 3 sts, work Ldc, dc in next 2 sts and in next ch-1 sp †, (2 dc, ch 2, 2 dc) in next 2-dc Cluster; repeat from ★ 2 times **more**, then repeat from † to † once; join with slip st to first dc: 60 dc.

Rnd 5: Ch 4, tr in next dc, (2 tr, ch 2, 2 tr) in next ch-2 sp, ★ tr in each dc across to next ch-2 sp, (2 tr, ch 2, 2 tr) in ch-2 sp; repeat from ★ 2 times **more**, tr in each dc across; join with slip st to first tr, finish off: 76 tr.

ASSEMBLY

With Black and using Placement Diagram as a guide, whipstitch Squares together forming 5 vertical strips of 7 Squares each *(Fig. 28a, page 142)*, beginning in second ch of first corner ch-2 and ending in first ch of next corner ch-2; then whipstitch strips together in same manner.

EDGING

With **right** side facing, join Black with slip st in any st; ch 1, sc evenly around working 3 sc in each corner; join with slip st to first sc, finish off.

PLACEMENT DIAGRAM

4	3	2	3	4
3	2	1	2	3
4	1	2	1	4
3	2	1	2	3
4	1	2	1	4
1	3	1	3	1
4	2	3	2	4

GOLDEN RULE Continued from page 94.

Row 5: With **right** side facing, join next color with slip st in first sc; ch 2, (dc in next sc, ch 1) 4 times, ★ † working **behind** Picot, (dc, ch 3, dc) in ch-3 sp one row **below** next Picot, ch 1, (dc in next sc, ch 1) 3 times †, YO, insert hook in next sc, YO and pull up a loop, YO and draw through 2 loops on hook, skip next sc, YO, insert hook in next sc, YO and pull up a loop, YO and draw through 2 loops on hook, YO and draw through all 3 loops on hook, ch 1, (dc in next sc, ch 1) 3 times; repeat from ★ 10 times **more**, then repeat from † to † once, skip next ch-1 sp, decrease: 108 sps.

Rows 6-158: Repeat Rows 2-5, 38 times; then repeat Row 2 once **more**; at end of Row 158, do **not** finish off.

Row 159: Ch 2, turn; skip first sc, (dc in next sc, ch 1) 4 times, ★ † working **behind** Picot, (dc, ch 3, dc) in ch-3 sp one row **below** next Picot, ch 1, (dc in next sc, ch 1) 3 times, skip next ch-1 sp, decrease †, ch 1, (dc in next sc, ch 1) 3 times; repeat from ★ 10 times **more**, then repeat from † to † once; do **not** finish off: 108 sps.

EDGING

Do **not** turn; work Picot; † working in end of rows, skip first dc row, (slip st, ch 2, dc) in next sc row, [skip next dc row, (slip st, ch 2, dc) in next sc row] across to last dc row, skip last dc row †; slip st in free loop of first ch *(Fig. 23b, page 140)*, ch 1, working over beginning ch, (slip st in next sp, ch 1) 9 times, [(slip st, ch 1) twice in next sp, (slip st in next sp, ch 1) 8 times] 11 times, slip st in free loop of next ch, ch 1, repeat from † to † once; working across Row 159, slip st in first dc, ch 1, (slip st in next ch-1 sp, ch 1) 4 times, (slip st, ch 1) twice in next ch-3 sp, [(slip st in next ch-1 sp, ch 1) 8 times, (slip st, ch 1) twice in next ch-3 sp] 11 times, (slip st in next sp, ch 1) 4 times; join with slip st to base of first ch-3, finish off.

RODEO STARS Continued from page 96.

ASSEMBLY

Lay out Panels with **right** sides facing and all marked edges at top. Whipstitch Panels together *(Fig. 28a, page 142)*, beginning in center dc of first corner and ending in center dc of next corner.

BORDER

With **right** side facing, join yarn with slip st in top right corner; ch 2, YO, insert hook in **same** st, YO and pull up a loop, YO, insert hook in next dc, YO and pull up a loop, YO and draw through all 5 loops on hook, ch 2, ★ YO, insert hook in **same** st as last loop of last st, YO and pull up a loop, YO, insert hook in next dc, YO and pull up a loop, YO and draw through all 5 loops on hook, ch 2; repeat from ★ around skipping joinings and working last half of last st in same st as beginning ch-2; join with slip st to first st, finish off.

Rnd 13: With **right** side facing, join Dk Rose with slip st in any corner ch-3 sp; ch 3, (dc, ch 3, 2 dc) in same sp, dc in each dc and in each Popcorn across to next corner ch-3 sp, ★ (2 dc, ch 3, 2 dc) in corner ch-3 sp, dc in each dc and in each Popcorn across to next corner ch-3 sp; repeat from ★ around; join with slip st to first dc, finish off: 120 dc.

Rnd 14: With **right** side facing, join Taupe with slip st in any corner ch-3 sp; ch 3, (dc, ch 3, 2 dc) in same sp, dc in next dc, work Popcorn, (dc in next 2 dc, work Popcorn) 9 times, dc in next dc, ★ (2 dc, ch 3, 2 dc) in next corner ch-3 sp, dc in next dc, work Popcorn, (dc in next 2 dc, work Popcorn) 9 times, dc in next dc; repeat from ★ around; join with slip st to first dc, finish off: 40 Popcorns.

Rnd 15: With **right** side facing, join Black with slip st in any corner ch-3 sp; ch 3, (dc, ch 3, 2 dc) in same sp, dc in each dc and in each Popcorn across to next corner ch-3 sp, ★ (2 dc, ch 3, 2 dc) in corner ch-3 sp, dc in each dc and in each Popcorn across to next corner ch-3 sp; repeat from ★ around; join with slip st to first dc, finish off: 152 dc.

Rnd 16: With **right** side facing, join Green with slip st in any corner ch-3 sp; ch 3, (2 dc, ch 2, 3 dc) in same sp, skip next 2 dc, (3 dc in next dc, skip next 2 dc) across to next corner ch-3 sp, ★ (3 dc, ch 2, 3 dc) in corner ch-3 sp, skip next 2 dc, (3 dc in next dc, skip next 2 dc) across to next corner ch-3 sp; repeat from ★ around; join with slip st to first dc, finish off: 56 3-dc groups.

Rnd 17: With **right** side facing, join Dk Green with slip st in any corner ch-2 sp; ch 3, (2 dc, ch 2, 3 dc) in same sp, (skip next 3 dc, 3 dc in sp **before** next 3-dc group) across to next corner ch-2 sp *(Fig. 26, page 141)*, ★ (3 dc, ch 2, 3 dc) in corner ch-2 sp, (skip next 3 dc, 3 dc in sp **before** next 3-dc group) across to next corner ch-2 sp; repeat from ★ around; join with slip st to first dc, finish off: 60 3-dc groups.

Rnd 18: With **right** side facing, join Black with slip st in any corner ch-2 sp; ch 1, (3 sc, ch 2, 3 sc) in same sp, sc in each dc across to next corner ch-2 sp, ★ (3 sc, ch 2, 3 sc) in corner ch-2 sp, sc in each dc across to next corner ch-2 sp; repeat from ★ around; join with slip st to first sc: 204 sc.

Rnd 19: Slip st in next 2 sc, ★ (slip st, ch 5) twice in next corner ch-2 sp, skip next 3 sc, (slip st in next sc, ch 5, skip next 3 sc) across to next corner ch-2 sp; repeat from ★ around; join with slip st to first corner st, finish off: 56 loops.

SQUARE JOINING

Join Squares together, forming 3 vertical strips of 4 Squares each as follows:

Holding 2 Squares with **right** sides together and working through **both** thicknesses, join Black with slip st in corner loop, ch 3, (slip st in next loop, ch 3) across to next corner loop, slip st in corner loop; finish off.

Note: There will be one Square unjoined to be used for pocket.

STRIP JOINING

To form pocket, place **right** side of remaining Square against **wrong** side of either end Square on center strip. Holding 2 strips with **right** sides together and working through **all** 3 thicknesses along pocket, join Black with slip st in corner loop; ch 3, (slip st in next loop, ch 3) across to next corner loop, slip st in corner loop; finish off.

Repeat for remaining strip.

BORDER

Note: Join bottom of pocket to Afghan by working through loops of **both** Squares as Border is worked.

With **right** side facing, join Black with slip st in any corner loop; ch 1, ★ (3 sc, ch 2, 3 sc) in corner loop, ch 1, (3 sc in next loop, ch 1) across to next corner loop; repeat from ★ around; join with slip st to first sc, finish off.

FOLDING

To form Pillowghan, spread Afghan with **right** side facing. Fold two outside strips **over** center strip, then fold in quarters **over** pocket. Invert the pocket **over** folded Afghan to form pillow *(Fig. 1)*.

Fig. 1

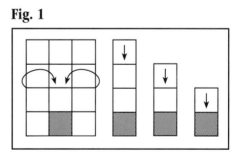

AUTUMN BLAZE

Ablaze with autumn hues, the squares of this cozy throw are created with simple double crochet stitches and chain spaces. Working rows on two sides of the beginning square produces the dramatic shadow effect.

COLOR SEQUENCE

2 Rnds Brown, 2 rows Dk Rust, 2 rows Rust, 2 rows Dk Tan, 2 rows Tan, and 2 rows Off-White.

SQUARE (Make 63)

With Brown, ch 6; join with slip st to form a ring.

Rnd 1 (Right side): Ch 3 **(counts as first dc, now and throughout)**, 2 dc in ring, (ch 2, 3 dc in ring) 3 times, hdc in first dc to form last sp: 12 dc.

Note: Loop a short piece of yarn around any stitch to mark last round as **right** side.

Rnd 2: Ch 3, (2 dc, ch 2, 3 dc) in same sp, ch 1, ★ (3 dc, ch 2, 3 dc) in next ch-2 sp, ch 1; repeat from ★ around; join with slip st to first dc, finish off: 24 dc.

Note: Begin working in rows.

Row 1: With **right** side facing, join Dk Rust with slip st in any corner ch-2 sp; ch 3, 2 dc in same sp, ch 1, 3 dc in next ch-1 sp, ch 1, (3 dc, ch 2, 3 dc) in next corner ch-2 sp, ch 1, 3 dc in next ch-1 sp, ch 1, 3 dc in next corner ch-2 sp, leave remaining sts unworked: 18 dc.

Row 2: Ch 4 **(counts as first dc plus ch 1, now and throughout)**, turn; (3 dc in next ch-1 sp, ch 1) twice, (3 dc, ch 2, 3 dc) in next corner ch-2 sp, ch 1, (3 dc in next ch-1 sp, ch 1) twice, skip next 2 dc, dc in last dc; finish off: 20 dc.

Row 3: With **right** side facing, join next color with slip st in first dc; ch 3, 2 dc in first ch-1 sp, ch 1, (3 dc in next ch-1 sp, ch 1) across to next corner ch-2 sp, (3 dc, ch 2, 3 dc) in corner ch-2 sp, ch 1, (3 dc in next ch-1 sp, ch 1) across to last sp, 2 dc in last sp, dc in last dc: 24 dc.

Row 4: Ch 4, turn; (3 dc in next ch-1 sp, ch 1) across to next corner ch-2 sp, (3 dc, ch 2, 3 dc) in corner ch-2 sp, ch 1, (3 dc in next ch-1 sp, ch 1) across to last 3 dc, skip next 2 dc, dc in last dc; finish off: 26 dc.

Rows 5-10: Repeat Rows 3 and 4, 3 times; at end of Row 10, finish off leaving a long end for sewing: 44 dc.

ASSEMBLY

With Rnds 1 and 2 at lower right corner, working in end of rows and through inside loops of sts and using yarn end, whipstitch Squares together, forming 7 vertical strips of 9 Squares each **(Fig. 28b, page 142)**; then with Off-White, whipstitch strips together in same manner.

Finished Size: 52" x 67"

MATERIALS

Worsted Weight Yarn:
- Brown - 10 ounces, (280 grams, 565 yards)
- Dk Rust - 7 ounces, (200 grams, 395 yards)
- Rust - 9 ounces, (260 grams, 510 yards)
- Dk Tan - 10 ounces, (280 grams, 565 yards)
- Tan - 12 ounces, (340 grams, 675 yards)
- Off-White - 13 ounces, (370 grams, 735 yards)

Crochet hook, size H (5.00 mm) **or** size needed for gauge

Yarn needle

GAUGE: Each Square = 7¼"

EDGING

Rnd 1: With **right** side facing, join Brown with slip st in any corner sp; ch 3, 2 dc in same sp, ch 1, (3 dc in next sp, ch 1) across to next corner sp, ★ (3 dc, ch 2, 3 dc) in corner sp, ch 1, (3 dc in next sp, ch 1) across to next corner sp; repeat from ★ around, 3 dc in same sp as first dc, hdc in first dc to form last sp.

Rnd 2: Ch 3, (2 dc, ch 2, 3 dc) in same sp, ch 1, (3 dc in next ch-1 sp, ch 1) across to next corner ch-2 sp, ★ (3 dc, ch 2, 3 dc) in corner ch-2 sp, ch 1, (3 dc in next ch-1 sp, ch 1) across to next corner ch-2 sp; repeat from ★ around; join with slip st to first dc, finish off.

WARM TRADITION

A handsome touch for the den, this manly throw features soothing neutral tones. The classic houndstooth pattern develops when you change yarn colors within the rows of easy single crochets. For a final touch, a unique "woven" edging is added by working chain loops around chain spaces.

Finished Size: 51" x 74"

MATERIALS
Worsted Weight Yarn:
Black - 40 ounces, (1,140 grams, 2,745 yards)
Brown - 34 ounces, (970 grams, 2,335 yards)
Crochet hook, size G (4.00 mm) **or** size needed for gauge

GAUGE: In pattern, 16 sc and 15 rows = 4"

With Black, ch 199 **loosely**.

Row 1: Sc in second ch from hook and in each ch across: 198 sc.

Note: When changing colors *(Fig. 24a, page 140)*, work over unused color, holding it with normal tension and keeping yarn to **wrong** side. Do not cut yarn unless specified.

Row 2 (Right side): Ch 1, turn; sc in first 3 sc changing to Brown in last sc, sc in next 2 sc changing to Black in last sc, ★ sc in next 5 sc changing to Brown in last sc, sc in next 2 sc changing to Black in last sc; repeat from ★ across to last 4 sc, sc in last 4 sc.

Note: Loop a short piece of yarn around any stitch to mark last row as **right** side.

Row 3: Ch 1, turn; sc in first 4 sc, with Brown sc in next 2 sc, ★ with Black sc in next 5 sc, with Brown sc in next 2 sc; repeat from ★ across to last 3 sc, with Black sc in last 3 sc.

Row 4: Ch 1, turn; sc in first 3 sc, with Brown sc in next 5 sc, ★ with Black sc in next 2 sc, with Brown sc in next 5 sc; repeat from ★ across to last sc, with Black sc in last sc.

Rows 5 and 6: Ch 1, turn; sc in first sc, with Brown sc in next 5 sc, ★ with Black sc in next 2 sc, with Brown sc in next 5 sc; repeat from ★ across to last 3 sc, with Black sc in last 3 sc.

Row 7: Ch 1, turn; sc in first 3 sc, with Brown sc in next 5 sc, ★ with Black sc in next 2 sc, with Brown sc in next 5 sc; repeat from ★ across to last sc, with Black sc in last sc.

Row 8: Ch 1, turn; sc in first 4 sc, with Brown sc in next 2 sc, ★ with Black sc in next 5 sc, with Brown sc in next 2 sc; repeat from ★ across to last 3 sc, with Black sc in last 3 sc.

Row 9: Ch 1, turn; sc in first 3 sc, with Brown sc in next 2 sc, ★ with Black sc in next 5 sc, with Brown sc in next 2 sc; repeat from ★ across to last 4 sc, with Black sc in last 4 sc.

Row 10: Ch 1, turn; sc in first 3 sc, with Brown sc in next 2 sc, ★ with Black sc in next 5 sc, with Brown sc in next 2 sc; repeat from ★ across to last 4 sc, with Black sc in last 4 sc.

Rows 11-273: Repeat Rows 3-10, 32 times; then repeat Rows 3-9 once **more**; at the end of Row 273, cut Brown.

Row 274: Ch 1, turn; sc in each sc across; do **not** finish off.

EDGING

Rnd 1: Ch 1, do **not** turn; 2 sc in last sc on Row 274; work 291 sc evenly spaced across end of rows; working in free loops of beginning ch *(Fig. 23b, page 140)*, 3 sc in first ch, 2 sc in next ch, sc in each ch across to last 2 chs, 2 sc in next ch, 3 sc in last ch; work 291 sc evenly spaced across end of rows; working across Row 274, 3 sc in first sc, 2 sc in next sc, sc in each sc across to last sc, 2 sc in last sc, sc in same st as first sc; join with slip st to first sc: 990 sc.

Rnd 2: Ch 1, (sc, ch 3, sc) in same st, ch 3, (skip next 2 sc, sc in next sc, ch 3) across to within 2 sc of center sc of next corner, skip next 2 sc, ★ (sc, ch 3, sc) in center sc, ch 3, (skip next 2 sc, sc in next sc, ch 3) across to within 2 sc of center sc of next corner, skip next 2 sc; repeat from ★ around; join with slip st to first sc, finish off.

Rnd 3: With **right** side facing, join Brown with slip st in any ch-3 sp; ch 3, ★ drop loop from hook, insert hook in next ch-3 sp, hook dropped loop and draw through to right side, ch 4; repeat from ★ around; join with slip st to first slip st, finish off.

CAMPFIRE BLANKET

An evening by the campfire is the perfect setting for this Navaho-look spread. Its zigzagging stripes are formed by working split treble crochets into the chain spaces of previous rows.

Finished Size: 46" x 62"

MATERIALS
Worsted Weight Yarn:
Scraps - 42 ounces, (1,190 grams, 2,760 yards)
Crochet hook, size I (5.50 mm) **or** size needed
for gauge

GAUGE: In pattern, 15 sts and 9 rows = 4"

STITCH GUIDE

BEGINNING SPLIT TR
YO, insert hook in first ch-1 sp, YO and pull up a loop (3 loops on hook), insert hook in skipped st one row **below** ch-1 *(Fig. 1a)*, YO and pull up a loop (4 loops on hook), insert hook in same ch-1 sp *(Fig. 1b)*, YO and draw through ch-1 sp **and** 2 loops on hook, (YO and draw through 2 loops on hook) twice *(Figs. 1c & d)*.

Fig. 1a

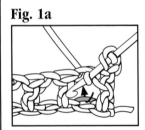

Fig. 1b

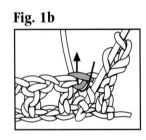

Fig. 1c

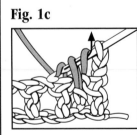

Fig. 1d

SPLIT TR
YO, insert hook in same ch-1 sp, YO and pull up a loop (3 loops on hook), insert hook in skipped st one row **below** ch-1, YO and pull up a loop (4 loops on hook), insert hook in same ch-1 sp, YO and draw through ch-1 sp **and** 2 loops on hook, (YO and draw through 2 loops on hook) twice.

Note: Change colors as desired *(Fig. 24a, page 140)*.

With first color, ch 174 **loosely**.
Row 1: Place marker in first ch from hook to mark ch-1 sp, place marker in fifth ch from hook to mark skipped st, dc in sixth ch from hook, (ch 1, skip next ch, dc in next ch) across: 85 ch-1 sps.
Row 2 (Right side): Ch 3 **(counts as first dc, now and throughout)**, turn; work beginning Split tr, (dc in next ch-1 sp, work Split tr) across to beginning ch, dc in top of beginning ch: 171 sts.
Note: Loop a short piece of yarn around any stitch to mark last row as **right** side.
Row 3: Ch 4 **(counts as first dc plus ch 1, now and throughout)**, turn; skip next st, dc in next dc, (ch 1, skip next st, dc in next dc) across: 85 ch-1 sps.
Row 4: Ch 3, turn; work beginning Split tr, (dc in next ch-1 sp, work Split tr) across to last dc, dc in last dc: 171 sts.
Repeat Rows 3 and 4 until Afghan measures 59¹/₂" from beginning ch ending by working Row 4.
Finish off.

EDGING
Rnd 1: With **right** side facing, join yarn with slip st in any corner; ch 1, sc evenly around working 3 sc in each corner; join with slip st to first sc.
Rnds 2-5: Ch 1, sc in each sc around working 3 sc in center sc of each corner; join with slip st to first sc.
Rnd 6: Ch 1, working from **left** to **right**, work reverse sc in each sc around *(Figs. 17a-d, page 138)*; join with slip st to first st, finish off.

111

MAGNIFICENT MUMS

The fiery flowers of fall are preserved on this beautiful chrysanthemum motif afghan. Surrounded by double and treble cluster leaves, the petals are formed with treble crochets and chains. For a lacy edging, each block is completed with rounds of loops and a simple border.

Finished Size: 37" x 55"

MATERIALS
Worsted Weight Yarn:
Tan - 17½ ounces, (500 grams, 990 yards)
Off-White - 17½ ounces, (500 grams, 990 yards)
Rust - 14 ounces, (400 grams, 795 yards)
Green - 7 ounces, (200 grams, 400 yards)
Crochet hook, size I (5.50 mm) **or** size needed
for gauge
Yarn needle

GAUGE: Rnd 1 = 2½"
Each Square = 9"

SQUARE (Make 24)

With Rust, ch 5; join with slip st to form a ring.
Rnd 1 (Right side): (Ch 3, tr, ch 3, slip st) 6 times in ring: 6 Petals.
Note: Loop a short piece of yarn around any stitch to mark last round as **right** side.
Rnd 2: (Ch 4, working **behind** Petals, slip st in st between next 2 Petals) around: 6 ch-4 sps.
Rnd 3: ★ Slip st in next ch-4 sp, (ch 3, tr, ch 3, slip st) twice in same sp; repeat from ★ around: 12 Petals.
Rnd 4: (Ch 6, working **behind** Petals, skip next 2 Petals, slip st in st **before** next Petal) around: 6 loops.
Rnd 5: ★ Slip st in next loop, (ch 3, 2 tr, ch 3, slip st) twice in same loop; repeat from ★ around: 12 Petals.
Rnd 6: (Ch 4, working **behind** Petals, slip st in st **before** next Petal) around; finish off: 12 ch-4 sps.
Note #1: To work **Double Crochet Cluster** *(abbreviated dc Cluster)*, ★ YO, insert hook in sp indicated, YO and pull up a loop, YO and draw through 2 loops on hook; repeat from ★ 2 times **more**, YO and draw through all 4 loops on hook *(Figs. 9a & b, page 137)*.
Note #2: To work **Treble Crochet Cluster** *(abbreviated tr Cluster)*, ★ YO twice, insert hook in sp indicated, YO and pull up a loop, (YO and draw through 2 loops on hook) twice; repeat from ★ 2 times **more**, YO and draw through all 4 loops on hook.

Rnd 7: With **right** side facing, join Green with slip st in any ch-4 sp; ch 1, sc in same sp, ch 4, sc in next ch-4 sp, ch 4, work (dc Cluster, ch 4, tr Cluster, ch 4, dc Cluster) in next ch-4 sp, ch 4, ★ (sc in next ch-4 sp, ch 4) twice, work (dc Cluster, ch 4, tr Cluster, ch 4, dc Cluster) in next ch-4 sp, ch 4; repeat from ★ 2 times **more**; join with slip st to first sc, finish off.
Rnd 8: With **right** side facing, join Off-White with slip st in any corner tr Cluster; ch 1, (sc, ch 4) twice in same st, (sc in next ch-4 sp, ch 4) across to next corner tr Cluster, ★ (sc, ch 4) twice in corner tr Cluster, (sc in next ch-4 sp, ch 4) across to next corner tr Cluster; repeat from ★ around; join with slip st to first sc: 28 ch-4 sps.
Rnd 9: Slip st in first corner ch-4 sp, ch 1, (sc, ch 4) twice in same sp, (sc in next ch-4 sp, ch 4) across to next corner ch-4 sp, ★ (sc, ch 4) twice in corner ch-4 sp, (sc in next ch-4 sp, ch 4) across to next corner ch-4 sp; repeat from ★ around; join with slip st to first sc: 32 ch-4 sps.
Rnd 10: Slip st in first corner ch-4 sp, ch 3 **(counts as first dc, now and throughout)**, (dc, ch 3, 2 dc) in same sp, 3 dc in each ch-4 sp across to next corner ch-4 sp, ★ (2 dc, ch 3, 2 dc) in corner ch-4 sp, 3 dc in each ch-4 sp across to next corner ch-4 sp; repeat from ★ around; join with slip st to first dc, finish off: 100 dc.
Rnd 11: With **right** side facing, join Tan with slip st in any corner ch-3 sp; ch 3, (dc, ch 3, 2 dc) in same sp, dc in each dc across to next corner ch-3 sp, ★ (2 dc, ch 3, 2 dc) in corner ch-3 sp, dc in each dc across to next corner ch-3 sp; repeat from ★ around; join with slip st to first dc, finish off: 116 dc.

ASSEMBLY

Using Tan, whipstitch Squares together, forming 4 vertical strips of 6 Squares each *(Fig. 28b, page 142)*, beginning in center ch of first corner and ending in center ch of next corner; then whipstitch strips together in same manner.

EDGING

With **right** side facing, join Tan with slip st in any corner ch-3 sp; ch 3, (dc, ch 3, 2 dc) in same sp, dc in each dc and in each ch and joining across to next corner ch-3 sp, ★ (2 dc, ch 3, 2 dc) in corner ch-3 sp, dc in each dc and in each ch and joining across to next corner ch-3 sp; repeat from ★ around; join with slip st to first dc, finish off.

RICH FALL STRIPES

Reflecting the brilliant shades of fall, the rich stripes of this snuggly throw are made with double crochets and front post treble stitches worked into the row below. To complete the set, the pattern is repeated on a coordinating pillow.

MATERIALS
Worsted Weight Yarn:
Green - 24¹/₂ ounces,
(700 grams, 1,680 yards)
Rust - 21 ounces,
(600 grams, 1,440 yards)
Gold - 10¹/₂ ounces,
(300 grams, 720 yards)
Brown - 10¹/₂ ounces,
(300 grams, 720 yards)
Crochet hook, size I (5.50 mm) **or** size needed for gauge
12" x 12" Pillow form
Yarn needle

GAUGE: In pattern, 13 dc and 8 rows = 4"

AFGHAN
Finished Size: 54" x 73"

COLOR SEQUENCE
2 Rows **each**: (Rust, Gold, Rust, Green, Brown, Green) 12 times.

With Rust, ch 173 **loosely**.
Row 1 (Right side)**:** Dc in fourth ch from hook and in each ch across: 171 sts.
Note: Loop a short piece of yarn around any stitch to mark last row as **right** side.
Row 2: Ch 3 **(counts as first dc, now and throughout)**, turn; dc in next dc and in each st across; finish off.
Note: To work **Front Post treble crochet (abbreviated FPtr)**, YO twice, insert hook from **front** to **back** around post of st indicated, YO and pull up a loop *(Fig. 15, page 138)*, (YO and draw through 2 loops on hook) 3 times. Skip st behind FPtr.
Row 3: With **right** side facing, join next color with slip st in first dc; ch 3, dc in next 3 dc, work FPtr around next dc, (dc in next 5 dc, work FPtr around next dc) across to last 4 dc, dc in last 4 dc: 28 FPtr.
Row 4: Ch 3, turn; dc in next dc and in each st across; finish off.
Row 5: With **right** side facing, join next color with slip st in first dc; ch 3, work FPtr around next dc, (dc in next 5 dc, work FPtr around next dc) across to last dc, dc in last dc: 29 FPtr.
Row 6: Ch 3, turn; dc in next FPtr and in each st across; finish off.
Rows 7-144: Repeat Rows 3-6, 34 times; then repeat Rows 3 and 4 once **more**; at end of Row 144, do **not** finish off.

EDGING
Rnd 1: Ch 1, turn; 3 sc in first dc, sc in each dc across to last dc, 3 sc in last dc; sc evenly across end of rows; working in free loops of beginning ch *(Fig. 23b, page 140)*, 3 sc in first ch, sc in each ch across to next corner, 3 sc in corner ch; sc evenly across end of rows; join with slip st to first sc.
Rnd 2: Ch 1, turn; sc in each sc around working 3 sc in each corner sc; join with slip st to first sc, finish off.

114

PILLOW

COLOR SEQUENCE
2 Rows **each**: (Rust, Gold, Rust, Green, Brown, Green) twice.

FRONT & BACK
With Rust, ch 41 **loosely**.

Rows 1-6: Work same as Afghan: 39 sts.

Rows 7-24: Repeat Rows 3-6, 4 times; then repeat Rows 3 and 4 once **more**; at end of Row 24, do **not** finish off.

EDGING

Rnd 1: Ch 1, turn; 3 sc in first dc, sc in each dc across to last dc, 3 sc in last dc; work 37 sc evenly spaced across end of rows; working in free loops of beginning ch, 3 sc in first ch, sc in each ch across to last ch, 3 sc in last ch; work 37 sc evenly spaced across end of rows; join with slip st to first sc, finish off.

ASSEMBLY
Place both pieces with **wrong** sides together. Whipstitch pieces together *(Fig. 28b, page 142)*, inserting pillow form before closing.

HAYRIDE WRAP

Although it appears to be made in panels, this afghan is really worked across its length with a pleasing pattern of V-stitches and single crochets. Completed with a simple border, the throw makes a wonderful accessory for an old-fashioned hayride.

Finished Size: 48" x 65"

MATERIALS

Worsted Weight Yarn:
    Tan - 22 ounces, (620 grams, 1,385 yards)
    Lt Tan - 13 ounces, (370 grams, 820 yards)
    Ecru - 13 ounces, (370 grams, 820 yards)
Crochet hook, size J (6.00 mm) **or** size needed
    for gauge

GAUGE: In pattern, sc, (ch 1, V-St, ch 1, sc) twice and
        Rows 1-10 = 4"

Note: Each row is worked across length of Afghan.

With Tan, ch 210 **loosely**.
Row 1 (Right side)**:** Sc in second ch from hook and in each ch across: 209 sc.
Note #1: Loop a short piece of yarn around any stitch to mark last row as **right** side.
Note #2: To work **V-St**, (dc, ch 1, dc) in next sc.
Row 2: Ch 2, turn; skip first sc, sc in next sc, ch 1, skip next 2 sc, work V-St, ★ ch 1, skip next 2 sc, sc in next sc, ch 1, skip next 2 sc, work V-St; repeat from ★ across: 35 V-Sts.
Rows 3-7: Ch 2, turn; sc in first V-St (ch-1 sp), ch 1, work V-St, ★ ch 1, sc in next V-St, ch 1, work V-St; repeat from ★ across to turning ch, leave turning ch unworked.
Row 8: Ch 1, turn; sc in each st and in each ch-1 sp across to turning ch changing to Ecru in last sc *(Fig. 24a, page 140)*; cut Tan and leave turning ch unworked: 209 sc.
Rows 9 and 10: Ch 1, turn; sc in each sc across changing to Lt Tan in last sc on Row 10; cut Ecru.
Row 11: Ch 1, turn; sc in each sc across.
Row 12: Ch 2, turn; skip first sc, sc in next sc, ch 1, skip next 2 sc, work V-St, ★ ch 1, skip next 2 sc, sc in next sc, ch 1, skip next 2 sc, work V-St; repeat from ★ across: 35 V-Sts.

Row 13: Ch 2, turn; sc in first V-St, ch 1, work V-St, ★ ch 1, sc in next V-St, ch 1, work V-St; repeat from ★ across to turning ch, leave turning ch unworked.
Row 14: Ch 1, turn; sc in each st and in each ch-1 sp across to turning ch changing to Ecru in last sc; cut Lt Tan and leave turning ch unworked: 209 sc.
Rows 15 and 16: Ch 1, turn; sc in each sc across changing to Tan in last sc on Row 16; cut Ecru.
Row 17: Ch 1, turn; sc in each sc across.
Rows 18-120: Repeat Rows 2-17, 6 times; then repeat Rows 2-8 once **more**.

EDGING

Rnd 1: Ch 1, turn; sc in each sc across to last sc, (sc, ch 1, sc) in last sc; work 135 sc evenly spaced across end of rows; working in free loops of beginning ch *(Fig. 23b, page 140)*, (sc, ch 1, sc) in first ch, sc in next 207 chs, (sc, ch 1, sc) in last ch; work 135 sc evenly spaced across end of rows, sc in same st as first sc, ch 1; join with slip st to first sc: 692 sc.
Rnd 2: Turn; slip st in first ch-1 sp, ch 1, (sc, ch 1, sc) in same sp, sc in each sc around working (sc, ch 1, sc) in each corner ch-1 sp; join with slip st to first sc changing to Lt Tan; cut Ecru: 700 sc.
Rnd 3: Ch 3 **(counts as first dc, now and throughout)**, turn; dc in each sc around working (dc, ch 1, dc) in each corner ch-1 sp; join with slip st to first dc changing to Tan; cut Lt Tan: 708 dc.
Rnd 4: Ch 3, turn; dc in next dc and in each dc around working (dc, ch 1, dc) in each corner ch-1 sp; join with slip st to first dc changing to Ecru; cut Tan: 716 dc.
Rnd 5: Ch 1, turn; sc in same st, ch 3, skip next dc, (sc in next dc, ch 3, skip next st) around; join with slip st to first sc, finish off.

TEAM SPIRIT

This warm stadium wrap will chase away the autumn chill so you can root the home team on to victory! The granny squares are made with cluster stitches and chain spaces and then whipstitched together. Our all-American color scheme can easily be adapted to reflect your team colors.

Finished Size: 57" x 70"

MATERIALS
Worsted Weight Yarn:
Blue - 24 ounces, (680 grams, 1,580 yards)
Red - 19 ounces, (540 grams, 1,250 yards)
Beige - 12 ounces, (340 grams, 790 yards)
Crochet hook, size H (5.00 mm) **or** size needed for gauge
Yarn needle

GAUGE: Each Square = 6¼"

SQUARE (Make 99)
With Blue, ch 4; join with slip st to form a ring.
Rnd 1 (Right side)**:** Ch 4, (dc in ring, ch 1) 11 times; join with slip st to third ch of beginning ch-4, finish off: 12 ch-1 sps.
Note #1: Loop a short piece of yarn around any stitch to mark last round as **right** side.
Note #2: To work **beginning Cluster**, ch 2, ★ YO, insert hook in same sp, YO and pull up a loop, YO and draw through 2 loops on hook; repeat from ★ once **more**, YO and draw through all 3 loops on hook *(Figs. 9a & b, page 137).*
Note #3: To work **Cluster**, ★ YO, insert hook in sp indicated, YO and pull up a loop, YO and draw through 2 loops on hook; repeat from ★ 2 times **more**, YO and draw through all 4 loops on hook.
Rnd 2: With **right** side facing, join Red with slip st in any ch-1 sp; work beginning Cluster, ch 3, (work Cluster in next ch-1 sp, ch 3) around; join with slip st to top of beginning Cluster, finish off: 12 Clusters.
Rnd 3: With **right** side facing, join Blue with slip st in any ch-3 sp; ch 1, sc in same sp, ch 5, (sc in next ch-3 sp, ch 5) around; join with slip st to first sc, finish off: 12 loops.
Rnd 4: With **right** side facing, join Beige with slip st in any loop; ch 1, sc in same loop, ch 3, sc in next loop, ch 1, (5 dc, ch 3, 5 dc) in next loop (corner made), ch 1, ★ sc in next loop, ch 3, sc in next loop, ch 1, (5 dc, ch 3, 5 dc) in next loop, ch 1; repeat from ★ around; join with slip st to first sc, finish off.

Rnd 5: With **right** side facing, join Red with slip st in any corner ch-3 sp; ch 3 **(counts as first dc, now and throughout)**, (2 dc, ch 2, 3 dc) in same sp, skip next 2 dc, 3 dc in next dc, skip next 2 dc, 2 dc in each of next 3 sps, skip next 2 dc, 3 dc in next dc, skip next 2 dc, ★ (3 dc, ch 2, 3 dc) in next corner ch-3 sp, skip next 2 dc, 3 dc in next dc, skip next 2 dc, 2 dc in each of next 3 sps, skip next 2 dc, 3 dc in next dc, skip next 2 dc; repeat from ★ around; join with slip st to first dc, finish off: 18 dc **each** side.
Rnd 6: With **right** side facing, join Blue with slip st in any corner ch-2 sp; ch 3, (2 dc, ch 2, 3 dc) in same sp, ★ † (skip next 3 dc, 3 dc in sp **before** next dc) twice *(Fig. 26, page 141)*, (skip next 2 dc, 2 dc in sp **before** next dc) twice, skip next 2 dc, (3 dc in sp **before** next dc, skip next 3 dc) twice †, (3 dc, ch 2, 3 dc) in next corner ch-2 sp; repeat from ★ 2 times **more**, then repeat from † to † once; join with slip st to first dc, finish off: 22 dc **each** side.

ASSEMBLY
With Blue, whipstitch Squares together, forming 9 vertical strips of 11 Squares each *(Fig. 28b, page 142)*, beginning in second ch of first corner ch-2 and ending in first ch of next corner ch-2; then whipstitch strips together in same manner.

EDGING
Rnd 1: With **right** side facing, join Beige with slip st in any corner ch-2 sp; ch 1, (sc, ch 1, sc) in same sp, sc in each dc across Square, † sc in ch-1 sp before next joining, skip joining, sc in first ch-1 sp on next Square, sc in each dc across Square †, repeat from † to † across to next corner ch-2 sp, ★ (sc, ch 1, sc) in corner ch-2 sp, sc in each dc across Square, repeat from † to † across to next corner ch-2 sp; repeat from ★ around; join with slip st to first sc.
Rnd 2: Ch 1, sc in same st, 4 sc in corner ch-1 sp, ★ sc in each sc across to next corner ch-1 sp, 4 sc in corner ch-1 sp; repeat from ★ 2 times **more**, sc in each sc across; join with slip st to first sc, finish off.

HARVEST HOME

A bounty of glorious textures is gathered for this homey afghan. Its "twigs" of harvesttime hues are created by working front post double treble stitches over single and double crochets. The throw is edged with a latticework of double crochet groups.

Finished Size: 47" x 65"

MATERIALS

Worsted Weight Yarn:
  Beige - 34 ounces, (970 grams, 2,235 yards)
  Brown - 7¹/₂ ounces, (210 grams, 495 yards)
  Teal - 7¹/₂ ounces, (210 grams, 495 yards)
Crochet hook, size H (5.00 mm) **or** size needed
  for gauge

GAUGE: In pattern, 14 sts and 12 rows = 4"

Note #1: Each row is worked across length of Afghan.

Note #2: When instructed to change colors *(Fig. 24a, page 140)*, do **not** cut Beige; carry **loosely** along edge.

With Beige, ch 215 **loosely**.
Row 1 (Right side)**:** Sc in second ch from hook and in each ch across: 214 sc.
Note: Loop a short piece of yarn around any stitch to mark last row as **right** side.
Row 2: Ch 3 **(counts as first dc, now and throughout)**, turn; dc in next sc and in each sc across.
Row 3: Ch 1, turn; sc in each dc across.
Row 4: Ch 3, turn; dc in next sc and in each sc across changing to Brown in last dc, drop Beige.
Note: To work **Front Post double treble crochet (abbreviated FPdtr)**, YO 3 times, insert hook from **front** to **back** around post of st indicated, YO and pull up a loop *(Fig. 16, page 138)*, (YO and draw through 2 loops on hook) 4 times. Skip st behind FPdtr.
Row 5: Ch 1, turn; sc in first dc, skip first 4 dc 3 rows **below**, work FPdtr around next dc, ★ sc in next 3 dc, work FPdtr around fourth dc from last FPdtr made; repeat from ★ across to last 4 dc, sc in last 4 dc; finish off: 53 FPdtr.
Row 6: With **right** side facing, insert hook in first sc, with Beige, YO and pull up a loop, ch 1, sc in same st and in each st across.
Row 7: Ch 3, turn; dc in next sc and in each sc across.
Row 8: Ch 1, turn; sc in each dc across.

Row 9: Ch 3, turn; dc in next sc and in each sc across changing to Teal in last dc, drop Beige.
Rows 10-13: Repeat Rows 5-8.
Row 14: Ch 3, turn; dc in next sc and in each sc across changing to Brown in last dc, drop Beige.
Row 15: Ch 1, turn; sc in first 4 dc, work FPdtr around second dc 3 rows **below**, ★ sc in next 3 dc, work FPdtr around fourth dc from last FPdtr made; repeat from ★ across to last dc, sc in last dc; finish off.
Rows 16-19: Repeat Rows 6-9.
Row 20: Repeat Row 15.
Rows 21-23: Repeat Rows 6-8.
Row 24: Repeat Row 14.
Rows 25-141: Repeat Rows 5-24, 5 times; then repeat Rows 5-21 once **more**; do **not** finish off.

TOP BORDER

Row 1: Ch 1, do **not** turn; work 142 sc evenly spaced across end of rows (top of Afghan).
Row 2: Ch 3, turn; 2 dc in same st, (skip next 2 sc, 3 dc in next sc) across: 48 3-dc groups.
Rows 3 and 4: Ch 3, turn; work 3 dc in sp **before** each 3-dc group across *(Fig. 26, page 141)*, dc in last dc. Finish off.

BOTTOM BORDER

Row 1: With **right** side facing, join Beige with slip st in end of first row; ch 1, work 142 sc evenly spaced across end of rows.
Rows 2-4: Work same as Top Border. Finish off.

EDGING

First side: With **right** side facing, join Beige with slip st in end of last row of Bottom Border; ch 1, sc evenly across end of rows and in each sc across last row of Afghan; finish off.
Second side: With **right** side facing, join Beige with slip st in last row of Top Border; ch 1, sc evenly across end of rows and in free loops of beginning ch *(Fig. 23b, page 140)*; finish off.

EVERGREEN INSPIRATION

Inspired by holiday evergreens, this cuddly afghan gets its plush texture from easy popcorn stitches and openwork rows of treble crochets. Reverse single crochets create a simple edging.

Note: Each row is worked across length of Afghan.

Ch 171 **loosely**.

Row 1: Dc in fourth ch from hook and in each ch across **(3 skipped chs count as first dc)**: 169 dc.

Note: To work **Popcorn**, 5 dc in next dc, drop loop from hook, insert hook in first dc of 5-dc group, hook dropped loop and draw through *(Fig. 10b, page 137)*.

Row 2 (Right side)**:** Ch 3 **(counts as first dc, now and throughout)**, turn; dc in next dc, work Popcorn, (dc in next 3 dc, work Popcorn) across to last 2 dc, dc in last 2 dc: 42 Popcorns.

Row 3: Ch 3, turn; dc in next dc and in each st across: 169 dc.

Row 4: Ch 5 **(counts as first tr plus ch 1)**, turn; skip next dc, tr in next dc, (ch 1, skip next dc, tr in next dc) across: 85 tr.

Row 5: Ch 3, turn; dc in each ch-1 sp and in each tr across: 169 dc.

Rows 6-67: Repeat Rows 2-5, 15 times; then repeat Rows 2 and 3 once **more**.

Do **not** finish off.

EDGING

Rnd 1: Ch 1, turn; sc evenly around working 3 sc in each corner; join with slip st to first sc.

Rnd 2: Ch 1, do **not** turn; working from **left** to **right**, work reverse sc in each sc around *(Figs. 17a-d, page 138)*; join with slip st to first st, finish off.

Finished Size: 47" x 66"

MATERIALS
Worsted Weight Brushed Acrylic Yarn:
    49 ounces,
        (1,390 grams, 2,205 yards)
Crochet hook, size K (6.50 mm) **or** size
    needed for gauge

GAUGE: In pattern, 13 sts = 5" and
        8 rows = 5$^1/_2$"

BLANKET OF SNOW

A blanket of snowflake motifs, this lacy throw works up quickly holding two strands of yarn together. The openwork squares are joined as you go and complemented by a dainty picot edging.

Finished Size: 56" x 70"

MATERIALS

Worsted Weight Yarn:
56 ounces, (1,590 grams, 3,520 yards)
Crochet hook, size N (9.00 mm) **or** size needed for gauge

GAUGE: Rnds 1-3 = 6½"
Each Motif = 13½"

Note: Entire Afghan is worked holding two strands of yarn together.

FIRST MOTIF

Ch 5; join with slip st to form a ring.

Rnd 1 (Right side)**:** Ch 3 **(counts as first dc, now and throughout)**, 2 dc in ring, ch 3, (3 dc in ring, ch 3) 3 times; join with slip st to first dc: 12 dc.

Note: Loop a short piece of yarn around any stitch to mark last round as **right** side.

Rnd 2: Ch 3, 2 dc in same st, ch 6, skip next dc, 3 dc in next dc, ch 2, ★ 3 dc in next dc, ch 6, skip next dc, 3 dc in next dc, ch 2; repeat from ★ around; join with slip st to first dc: 24 dc and 4 ch-6 sps.

Rnd 3: Slip st in next dc, ch 3, 2 dc in same st, ch 4, sc in next ch-6 sp, ch 4, skip next dc, 3 dc in next dc, ch 2, skip next ch-2 sp and next dc, ★ 3 dc in next dc, ch 4, sc in next ch-6 sp, ch 4, skip next dc, 3 dc in next dc, ch 2, skip next ch-2 sp and next st; repeat from ★ around; join with slip st to first dc: 28 sts and 12 sps.

Rnd 4: Slip st in next dc, ch 3, 2 dc in same st, ch 4, sc in next ch-4 sp, sc in next sc and in next ch-4 sp, ch 4, skip next dc, 3 dc in next dc, ch 5, skip next ch-2 sp and next dc, ★ 3 dc in next dc, ch 4, sc in next ch-4 sp, sc in next sc and in next ch-4 sp, ch 4, skip next dc, 3 dc in next dc, ch 5, skip next ch-2 sp and next st; repeat from ★ around; join with slip st to first dc: 36 sts and 12 sps.

Rnd 5: Slip st in next dc, ch 3, 2 dc in same st, ch 3, sc in next ch-4 sp, sc in next 3 sc and in next ch-4 sp, ch 3, skip next dc, 3 dc in next dc, ch 5, dc in next ch-5 sp, ch 5, skip next dc, ★ 3 dc in next dc, ch 3, sc in next ch-4 sp, sc in next 3 sc and in next ch-4 sp, ch 3, skip next dc, 3 dc in next dc, ch 5, dc in next ch-5 sp, ch 5, skip next st; repeat from ★ around; join with slip st to first dc: 48 sts and 16 sps.

Rnd 6: Slip st in next dc, ch 3, 2 dc in same st, ch 3, skip next sc, sc in next 3 sc, ch 3, skip next dc, 3 dc in next dc, ch 2, dc in next ch-5 sp, ch 3, (dc, ch 5, dc) in next dc, ch 3, dc in next ch-5 sp, ch 2, skip next dc, ★ 3 dc in next dc, ch 3, skip next sc, sc in next 3 sc, ch 3, skip next dc, 3 dc in next dc, ch 2, dc in next ch-5 sp, ch 3, (dc, ch 5, dc) in next dc, ch 3, dc in next ch-5 sp, ch 2, skip next st; repeat from ★ around; join with slip st to first dc: 52 sts and 28 sps.

Rnd 7: Slip st in next dc, ch 3, 2 dc in same st, ch 3, skip next sc, sc in next sc, ch 3, skip next dc, 3 dc in next dc, ch 3, skip next dc, (dc in next dc, ch 3) twice, dc in next ch-5 sp, ch 3, (dc in next dc, ch 3) twice, skip next dc, ★ 3 dc in next dc, ch 3, skip next sc, sc in next sc, ch 3, skip next dc, 3 dc in next dc, ch 3, skip next dc, (dc in next dc, ch 3) twice, dc in next ch-5 sp, ch 3, (dc in next dc, ch 3) twice, skip next st; repeat from ★ around; join with slip st to first dc: 48 sts and 32 sps.

Rnd 8: Slip st in next dc, ch 3, 2 dc in same st, ch 3, sc in next sc, ch 3, skip next dc, 3 dc in next dc, ch 4, skip next dc, (sc in next dc, ch 4) twice, (dc, ch 5, dc) in next dc, ch 4, (sc in next dc, ch 4) twice, skip next dc, ★ 3 dc in next dc, ch 3, sc in next sc, ch 3, skip next dc, 3 dc in next dc, ch 4, skip next dc, (sc in next dc, ch 4) twice, (dc, ch 5, dc) in next dc, ch 4, (sc in next dc, ch 4) twice, skip next st; repeat from ★ around; join with slip st to first dc, finish off: 52 sts and 36 sps.

Continued on page 133.

COZY APPEAL

This appealing throw will keep you cozy when you curl up with a good book this winter! To create a checked pattern on one side and delightful stripes on the other, double crochet stitches are worked into the free loops of the preceding rows. Plush fringe adds a decorative finishing touch.

Finished Size: 52" x 70"

MATERIALS
Worsted Weight Yarn:
Cream - 26 ounces, (740 grams, 1,930 yards)
Lt Teal - 6 ounces, (170 grams, 445 yards)
Teal - 6 ounces, (170 grams, 445 yards)
Med Teal - 6 ounces, (170 grams, 445 yards)
Dk Teal - 6 ounces, (170 grams, 445 yards)
Crochet hook, size J (6.00 mm) **or** size needed
   for gauge

GAUGE: In pattern, 17 sts and 17 rows = 5"

COLOR SEQUENCE
5 Rows Cream, ★ 1 row each Lt Teal, Cream, Lt Teal, Teal, Cream, Teal, Med Teal, Cream, Med Teal, Dk Teal, Cream, Dk Teal; 5 rows Cream; repeat from ★ 9 times **more**.

Note #1: Each row is worked across length of Afghan.

Note #2: When joining yarn and finishing off, always leave a 7" end to be worked into fringe.

With Cream, ch 239 **loosely**.
Row 1 (Right side)**:** Sc in second ch from hook and in each ch across; finish off: 238 sc.
Note #1: Loop a short piece of yarn around any stitch to mark last row as **right** side.
Note #2: Work sc in Back Loops Only throughout *(Fig. 22, page 140)*.
Rows 2-5: With **right** side facing, join Cream with slip st in first sc; ch 1, sc in each sc across; finish off.
Row 6: With **right** side facing, join new color with slip st in first st; ch 1, sc in each st across; finish off.
Row 7: With **right** side facing, join Cream with slip st in first sc; ch 1, sc in same st, working in free loops *(Fig. 23a, page 140)*, dc in each sc in row **below** next 4 sc, ★ sc in next 4 sc, dc in each sc in row **below** next 4 sc; repeat from ★ across to last sc, sc in last sc; finish off: 30 4-dc groups.
Row 8: With **right** side facing, join new color with slip st in first sc; ch 1, sc in same st and in next 4 dc, dc in each sc in row **below** next 4 sc, ★ sc in next 4 dc, dc in each sc in row **below** next 4 sc; repeat from ★ across to last 5 sts, sc in last 5 sts; finish off.
Rows 9-17: Repeat Rows 6-8, 3 times.
Rows 18-22: With **right** side facing, join Cream with slip st in first sc; ch 1, sc in each st across; finish off.
Rows 23-175: Repeat Rows 6-22, 9 times.

Holding two strands of corresponding color together, add additional fringe across short edges of Afghan *(Figs. 29b & d, page 142)*.

MAJESTIC PINE

*Reflecting the regal beauty of majestic pines, this rich green afghan is
fast and easy to make using soft brushed acrylic yarn. Simple, airy
motifs are created with double crochet stitches and chain spaces, and
the blocks are whipstitched together and bordered with picots.*

Finished Size: 53" x 70"

MATERIALS
Worsted Weight Brushed Acrylic Yarn:
   46 ounces, (1,310 grams, 2,070 yards)
Crochet hook, size K (6.50 mm) **or** size needed
   for gauge
Yarn needle

GAUGE: Rnds 1 and 2 = 3"
   Each Square = 8½"

SQUARE (Make 48)
Ch 3; join with slip st to form a ring.
Rnd 1 (Right side)**:** Ch 3 **(counts as first dc, now and
throughout)**, 2 dc in ring, ch 3, (3 dc in ring, ch 3) 3 times;
join with slip st to first dc: 4 ch-3 sps and 12 dc.
Note: Loop a short piece of yarn around any stitch to mark last
round as **right** side.
Rnd 2: Slip st in next 2 dc and in next ch-3 sp, ch 3, (2 dc,
ch 3, 3 dc) in same sp, ch 1, ★ (3 dc, ch 3, 3 dc) in next
ch-3 sp, ch 1; repeat from ★ around; join with slip st to first dc:
8 sps and 24 dc.
Rnd 3: Slip st in next 2 dc and in next ch-3 sp, ch 3, (2 dc,
ch 3, 3 dc) in same sp, ch 2, dc in next ch-1 sp, ch 2, ★ (3 dc,
ch 3, 3 dc) in next ch-3 sp, ch 2, dc in next ch-1 sp, ch 2;
repeat from ★ around; join with slip st to first dc: 12 sps and
28 dc.
Rnds 4-7: Slip st in next 2 dc and in next ch-3 sp, ch 3, (2 dc,
ch 3, 3 dc) in same sp, ch 2, (dc in next ch-2 sp, ch 2) across
to next ch-3 sp, ★ (3 dc, ch 3, 3 dc) in ch-3 sp, ch 2, (dc in
next ch-2 sp, ch 2) across to next ch-3 sp; repeat from ★
around; join with slip st to first dc: 28 sps and 44 dc.
Finish off.

ASSEMBLY
Whipstitch Squares together forming 6 vertical strips of
8 Squares each *(Fig. 28b, page 142)*, beginning in center ch
of first corner and ending in center ch of next corner; then
whipstitch strips together in same manner.

EDGING
Rnd 1: With **right** side facing, join yarn with slip st in top right
corner ch-3 sp; ch 1, 3 sc in same sp, † work 152 sc evenly
spaced across to next corner ch-3 sp, 3 sc in corner ch-3 sp;
work 202 sc evenly spaced across to next corner ch-3 sp †, 3 sc
in corner ch-3 sp, repeat from † to † once; join with slip st to
first sc: 720 sc.
Note: To work **Picot,** ch 4, slip st in fourth ch from hook.
Rnd 2: Ch 1, sc in same st, work Picot, (skip next sc, sc in next
4 sc, work Picot) around to last 4 sc, skip next sc, sc in last
3 sc; join with slip st to first sc, finish off.

SIMPLE SNOWMAN

Holiday plans you'll conspire as you dream by the fire when wrapped in this jolly snowman afghan. To create the frosty friend, simple squares — made from clusters, double crochets, and chain spaces — are whipstitched together following our helpful placement diagram.

Finished Size: 48" x 59"

MATERIALS

Worsted Weight Yarn:
   Beige - 20 ounces, (570 grams, 1,255 yards)
   Blue - 17 ounces, (480 grams, 1,070 yards)
   Green - 2 ounces, (60 grams, 125 yards)
   Red - 13 ounces, (370 grams, 815 yards)
Crochet hook, size H (5.00 mm) **or** size needed
   for gauge
Yarn needle

GAUGE: Each Square = 2¼"

SQUARE A

Note: Make the number of Squares indicated with the following colors: Beige - 102, Blue - 151, Green - 14, and Red - 10.
Ch 4; join with slip st to form a ring.
Rnd 1 (Right side): Ch 4, (dc in ring, ch 1) 11 times; join with slip st to third ch of beginning ch-4: 12 ch-1 sps.
Note #1: Loop a short piece of yarn around any stitch to mark last round as **right** side.
Note #2: To work **Cluster**, ★ YO, insert hook in st or sp indicated, YO and pull up a loop, YO and draw through 2 loops on hook; repeat from ★ once **more**, YO and draw through all 3 loops on hook (*Figs. 9a & b, page 137*).
Rnd 2: Slip st in first ch-1 sp, ch 2, dc in same sp, ch 1, (work Cluster in next ch-1 sp, ch 1) twice, tr in next dc, ch 1, ★ (work Cluster in next ch-1 sp, ch 1) 3 times, tr in next dc, ch 1; repeat from ★ around; skip beginning ch-2 and join with slip st to first dc, finish off: 16 sts and 16 ch-1 sps.

SQUARE B (Make 13)

With Beige, ch 4; join with slip st to form a ring.
Rnd 1 (Right side): Ch 4, (dc in ring, ch 1) 11 times; join with slip st to third ch of beginning ch-4, finish off: 12 ch-1 sps.
Note: Mark last round as **right** side.
Rnd 2: With **right** side facing, join Blue with slip st in any ch-1 sp; ch 2, dc in same sp, ch 1, (work Cluster in next ch-1 sp, ch 1) twice, tr in next dc, ch 1, ★ (work Cluster in next ch-1 sp, ch 1) 3 times, tr in next dc, ch 1; repeat from ★ around; skip beginning ch-2 and join with slip st to first dc, finish off: 16 sts and 16 ch-1 sps.

SQUARE C (Make 10)

Note: When changing colors (*Figs. 24a & b, page 140*), do **not** cut yarn unless otherwise instructed.
With Beige, ch 4; join with slip st to form a ring.
Rnd 1 (Right side): Ch 4, dc in ring, (ch 1, dc in ring) 4 times changing to Blue in last dc, ch 1, (dc in ring, ch 1) 6 times; join with slip st to third ch of beginning ch-4 changing to Beige: 12 ch-1 sps.
Note: Mark last round as **right** side.
Rnd 2: Slip st in first ch-1 sp, ch 2, dc in same sp, ch 1, (work Cluster in next ch-1 sp, ch 1) twice, tr in next dc, (ch 1, work Cluster in next ch-1 sp) 3 times changing to Blue in last Cluster, ch 1, tr in next dc, ch 1, (work Cluster in next ch-1 sp, ch 1) 3 times, tr in next dc, (ch 1, work Cluster in next ch-1 sp) 3 times changing to Beige in last Cluster; cut Blue, ch 1, tr in next st, ch 1; skip beginning ch-2 and join with slip st to first dc, finish off: 16 sts and 16 ch-1 sps.

Continued on page 132.

Certificate of Quality Assurance

24K or 24KT	24 Karat Gold
18K or 18KT	18 Karat Gold
14K or 14KT	14 Karat Gold
10K or 10KT	10 Karat Gold
Sterling or 925	Sterling Silver
Plat.	Platinum

Each piece of jewelry presented on QVC is subject to strict standards of quality and workmanship established by our Quality Assurance Department. Through a systematic inspection program, the Quality Assurance Laboratory ensures that all the jewelry meets or exceeds those rigorous standards. The U.S. Government requires that all karat gold, sterling silver and platinum jewelry have a hallmark that accurately represents precious metal content. To ensure that hallmarks are accurate and comply with U.S. Government requirements, we assay samples of all karat gold, sterling silver and platinum jewelry sold by QVC.

Eric Christopher

Eric Christopher, Vice President, Quality Assurance

Corp. President

Thomas Barkowski

$$2\;)\;48.39$$

$$24.19\overline{2}$$

$$4$$

$$1209 \qquad 8$$
$$8$$

$$2\;)\;24.19.\tfrac{1}{2}. \qquad 3$$
$$2 \qquad\qquad\qquad 3$$

$$4 \qquad\qquad 19$$
$$4 \qquad\qquad 18$$
$$\quad 19$$
$$\quad 18$$

$$12\!\!\not{69}\;.06$$
$$8$$

$$3\;)\;24.19$$
$$24 \qquad 19$$
$$\qquad\quad 18$$

$$8.06$$
$$8.06$$
$$8.06$$

$$24.18 \qquad 8.06$$

SIMPLE SNOWMAN Continued from page 130.

ASSEMBLY

Using Placement Diagram as a guide, whipstitch Squares together forming 15 vertical strips of 20 Squares each *(Fig. 28a, page 142)*, beginning in tr of first corner and ending in tr of next corner; then whipstitch strips together in same manner.

PLACEMENT DIAGRAM

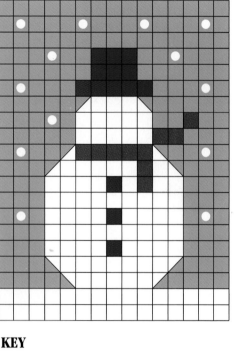

KEY

⊙ - Square B

◪ - Square C

BORDER

Rnd 1: With **right** side facing, join Red with slip st in any corner tr; ch 3, 2 dc in same st, ★ † dc in next ch-1 sp, (dc in next Cluster and in next ch-1 sp) 3 times, [dc in same st as joining, dc in joining and in same st as joining on next Square, dc in next ch-1 sp, (dc in next Cluster and in next ch-1 sp) 3 times] across to next corner tr †, 3 dc in corner tr; repeat from ★ 2 times **more**, then repeat from † to † once; join with slip st to top of beginning ch-3: 700 sts.

Rnd 2: Ch 3, (hdc, ch 1) twice in next dc, (hdc in next dc, ch 1, skip next dc) across to next corner 3-dc group, ★ hdc in next dc, ch 1, (hdc, ch 1) twice in next dc, (hdc in next dc, ch 1, skip next dc) across to next corner 3-dc group; repeat from ★ around; join with slip st to second ch of beginning ch-3: 358 sps.

Rnd 3: Ch 3, dc in each ch-1 sp and in each hdc around working 3 dc in each corner ch-1 sp; join with slip st to top of beginning ch-3: 724 sts.

Rnd 4: Slip st in next dc, ch 3, skip next dc, hdc in next dc, ch 1, (hdc, ch 1) twice in next dc, ★ (hdc in next dc, ch 1, skip next dc) across to next corner 3-dc group, hdc in next dc, ch 1, (hdc, ch 1) twice in next dc; repeat from ★ 2 times **more**, (hdc in next dc, ch 1, skip next st) across; join with slip st to second ch of beginning ch-3: 370 sps.

Rnd 5: Ch 3, dc in each ch-1 sp and in each hdc around working 3 dc in each corner ch-1 sp; join with slip st to top of beginning ch-3, finish off: 748 sts.

Rnd 6: With **right** side facing, join Beige with slip st in center dc of any corner; ch 2, dc in same sp, (ch 2, work Cluster in same st) twice, ch 1, skip next dc, (work Cluster in next dc, ch 1, skip next dc) across to center dc of next corner, ★ work Cluster in center dc, (ch 2, work Cluster in same st) twice, ch 1, skip next dc, (work Cluster in next dc, ch 1, skip next dc) across to center dc of next corner; repeat from ★ around; skip beginning ch-2 and join with slip st to first dc: 382 Clusters.

Rnd 7: Ch 2, dc in same st, ch 1, work Cluster in next Cluster, (ch 2, work Cluster in same st) twice, ch 1, ★ (work Cluster in next Cluster, ch 1) across to center Cluster of next corner, work Cluster in center Cluster, (ch 2, work Cluster in same st) twice, ch 1; repeat from ★ 2 times **more**, (work Cluster in next Cluster, ch 1) across; skip beginning ch-2 and join with slip st to first dc: 390 Clusters.

Rnds 8-10: Ch 2, dc in same st, ch 1, ★ (work Cluster in next Cluster, ch 1) across to center Cluster of next corner, work Cluster in center Cluster, (ch 2, work Cluster in same st) twice, ch 1; repeat from ★ 3 times **more**, (work Cluster in next Cluster, ch 1) across; skip beginning ch-2 and join with slip st to first dc; at end of Rnd 10, finish off: 414 Clusters.

Rnd 11: With **right** side facing, join Red with slip st in center Cluster of any corner; ch 3, 2 dc in same st, 2 dc in next ch-2 sp, ★ dc in each Cluster and in each ch-1 sp across to next ch-2 sp, 2 dc in ch-2 sp, 3 dc in next Cluster, 2 dc in next ch-2 sp; repeat from ★ 2 times **more**, dc in each Cluster and in each ch-1 sp across; join with slip st to top of beginning ch-3: 844 sts.

Rnds 12-15: Repeat Rnds 2-5.

BLANKET OF SNOW Continued from page 130.

ADDITIONAL MOTIFS

Work same as First Motif through Rnd 7; do **not** finish off: 48 sts and 32 sps.

Rnd 8: Work One or Two Side Joining arranging Motifs in 5 rows with 4 Motifs in each row.

ONE SIDE JOINING

Slip st in next dc, ch 3, 2 dc in same st, ch 3, sc in next sc, ch 3, skip next dc, 3 dc in next dc, ch 4, skip next dc, (sc in next dc, ch 4) twice, ★ (dc, ch 5, dc) in next dc, ch 4, (sc in next dc, ch 4) twice, skip next dc, 3 dc in next dc, ch 3, sc in next sc, ch 3, skip next dc, 3 dc in next dc, ch 4, skip next dc, (sc in next dc, ch 4) twice; repeat from ★ once **more**, dc in next dc, ch 2, holding Motifs with **wrong** sides together, slip st in corresponding corner ch-5 sp on **adjacent Motif** *(Fig. 25, page 140)*, ch 2, dc in same st on **new Motif**, (ch 1, slip st in next ch-4 sp on **adjacent Motif**, ch 2, sc in next dc on **new Motif**) twice, ch 4, skip next dc, 2 dc in next dc, ch 1, skip next dc on **adjacent Motif**, slip st in next dc, ch 1, slip st in top of last dc made on **new Motif**, dc in same st, ch 3, sc in next sc, ch 3, skip next dc, 2 dc in next dc, ch 1, skip next sc and next dc on **adjacent Motif**, slip st in next dc, ch 1, slip st in top of last dc made on **new Motif**, dc in same st, ch 4, skip next dc, sc in next dc, ch 1, skip next ch-4 sp on **adjacent Motif**, slip st in next ch-4 sp, ch 2, sc in next dc on **new Motif**, ch 1, slip st in next ch-4 sp on **adjacent Motif**, ch 2, dc in next dc on **new Motif**, ch 2, slip st in next corner ch-5 sp on **adjacent Motif**, ch 2, dc in same st on **new Motif**, ch 4, (sc in next dc, ch 4) twice; join with slip st to first dc, finish off.

TWO SIDE JOINING

Slip st in next dc, ch 3, 2 dc in same st, ch 3, sc in next sc, ch 3, skip next dc, 3 dc in next dc, ch 4, skip next dc, (sc in next dc, ch 4) twice, (dc, ch 5, dc) in next dc, ch 4, (sc in next dc, ch 4) twice, skip next dc, 3 dc in next dc, ch 3, sc in next sc, ch 3, skip next dc, 3 dc in next dc, ch 4, skip next dc, (sc in next dc, ch 4) twice, dc in next dc, ch 2, holding Motifs with **wrong** sides together, slip st in corresponding corner ch-5 sp on **adjacent Motif**, ch 2, † dc in same st on **new Motif**, (ch 1, slip st in next ch-4 sp on **adjacent Motif**, ch 2, sc in next dc on **new Motif**) twice, ch 4, skip next dc, 2 dc in next dc, ch 1, skip next dc on **adjacent Motif**, slip st in next dc, ch 1, slip st in top of last dc made on **new Motif**, dc in same st, ch 3, sc in next sc, ch 3, skip next dc, 2 dc in next dc, ch 1, skip next sc and next dc on **adjacent Motif**, slip st in next dc, ch 1, slip st in top of last dc made on **new Motif**, dc in same st, ch 4, skip next dc, sc in next dc, ch 1, skip next ch-4 sp on **adjacent Motif**, slip st in next ch-4 sp, ch 2, sc in next dc on **new Motif**, ch 1, slip st in next ch-4 sp on **adjacent Motif**, ch 2, dc in next dc on **new Motif** †, ch 1, (slip st in next corner ch-5 sp on **adjacent Motif**, ch 1) twice, repeat from † to † once, ch 2, slip st in next corner ch-5 sp on **adjacent Motif**, ch 2, dc in same st on **new Motif**, ch 4, (sc in next dc, ch 4) twice; join with slip st to first dc, finish off.

EDGING

Note: To work **Picot Loop**, ch 5, slip st in third ch from hook, ch 3.

With **right** side facing, join yarn with slip st in any corner ch-5 sp; ch 1, (sc, work Picot Loop, sc) in same sp, ★ † work Picot Loop, (sc in next sp, work Picot Loop) 3 times, (sc in center dc of next 3-dc group, work Picot Loop) twice, (sc in next sp, work Picot Loop) 3 times, [skip next sp, sc in next joining, work Picot Loop, skip next sp, (sc in next sp, work Picot Loop) 3 times, (sc in center dc of next 3-dc group, work Picot Loop) twice, (sc in next sp, work Picot Loop) 3 times] across to next corner ch-5 sp †, (sc, work Picot Loop, sc) in corner ch-5 sp; repeat from ★ 2 times **more**, then repeat from † to † once; join with slip st to first sc, finish off.

BASIC INFORMATION

ABBREVIATIONS

BPdc	Back Post double crochet(s)
ch(s)	chain(s)
dc	double crochet(s)
dk	dark
dtr	double treble crochet(s)
FPdc	Front Post double crochet(s)
FPdtr	Front Post double treble crochet(s)
FPtr	Front Post treble crochet(s)
hdc	half double crochet(s)
Ldc	Long double crochet(s)
lt	light
med	medium
mm	millimeters
Rnd(s)	Round(s)
sc	single crochet(s)
sp(s)	space(s)
st(s)	stitch(es)
tr	treble crochet(s)
YO	yarn over

SYMBOLS

★ — work instructions following ★ as many **more** times as indicated in addition to the first time.

† to † — work all instructions from first † to second † **as many** times as specified.

( ) or [ ] — work enclosed instructions **as many** times as specified by the number immediately following **or** work all enclosed instructions in the stitch or space indicated **or** contains explanatory remarks.

TERMS

chain loosely — work the chain **only** loose enough for the hook to pass through the chain easily when working the next row or round into the chain.

multiple — the number of stitches required to complete one repeat of a pattern.

post — the vertical shaft of a stitch.

right side vs. wrong side — the right side of your work is the side that will show when the piece is finished.

work across or around — continue working in the established pattern.

GAUGE

Gauge is the number of stitches and rows or rounds per inch and is used to determine the finished size of a project. All crochet patterns will specify the gauge that you must match to ensure proper size and to be sure you have enough yarn to complete the project.

Hook size given in instructions is merely a guide. Because everyone crochets differently — loosely, tightly, or somewhere in between — the finished size can vary, even when crocheters use the very same pattern, yarn, and hook.

Before beginning any crocheted item, it is absolutely necessary for you to crochet a gauge swatch in the pattern stitch indicated and with the weight of yarn and hook size suggested. Your swatch must be large enough to measure your gauge. Lay your swatch on a hard, smooth, flat surface. Then measure it, counting your stitches and rows or rounds carefully. If your swatch is smaller than specified or you have too many stitches per inch, try again with a larger size hook; if your swatch is larger or you don't have enough stitches per inch, try again with a smaller size hook. Keep trying until you find the size that will give you the specified gauge. DO NOT HESITATE TO CHANGE HOOK SIZE TO OBTAIN CORRECT GAUGE. Once proper gauge is obtained, measure width of piece approximately every 3" to be sure gauge remains consistent.

BASIC STITCH GUIDE

CHAIN (abbreviated ch)

To work a chain stitch, begin with a slip knot on the hook. Bring the yarn **over** hook from **back** to **front**, catching the yarn with the hook and turning the hook slightly toward you to keep the yarn from slipping off. Draw the yarn through the slip knot **(Fig. 1)**.

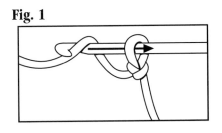

Fig. 1

WORKING INTO THE CHAIN

When beginning a first row of crochet in a chain, always skip the first chain from the hook, and work into the second chain from hook (for single crochet), third chain from hook (for half double crochet), or fourth chain from hook (for double crochet), etc. **(Fig. 2a)**.

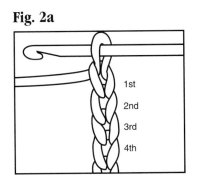

Fig. 2a

1st
2nd
3rd
4th

Method 1: Insert hook into back ridge of each chain indicated **(Fig. 2b)**.
Method 2: Insert hook under top two strands of each chain **(Fig. 2c)**.

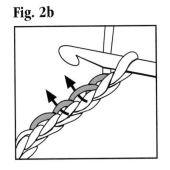

Fig. 2b

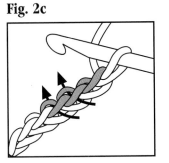

Fig. 2c

SLIP STITCH (abbreviated slip st)

This stitch is used to attach new yarn, to join work, or to move the yarn across a group of stitches without adding height. Insert hook in stitch or space indicated, YO and draw through stitch **and** loop on hook **(Fig. 3)**.

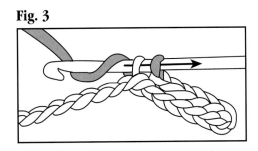

Fig. 3

SINGLE CROCHET (abbreviated sc)

Insert hook in stitch or space indicated, YO and pull up a loop, YO and draw through both loops on hook **(Fig. 4)**.

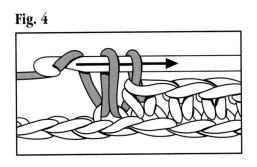

Fig. 4

HALF DOUBLE CROCHET
(abbreviated hdc)

YO, insert hook in stitch or space indicated, YO and pull up a loop, YO and draw through all 3 loops on hook *(Fig. 5)*.

Fig. 5

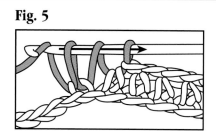

DOUBLE CROCHET *(abbreviated dc)*

YO, insert hook in stitch or space indicated, YO and pull up a loop, YO and draw through 2 loops on hook *(Fig. 6a)*, YO and draw through remaining 2 loops on hook *(Fig. 6b)*.

Fig. 6a

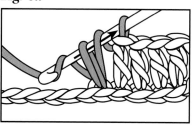

Fig. 6b

TREBLE CROCHET *(abbreviated tr)*

YO twice, insert hook in stitch or space indicated, YO and pull up a loop *(Fig. 7a)*, (YO and draw through 2 loops on hook) 3 times *(Fig. 7b)*.

Fig. 7a

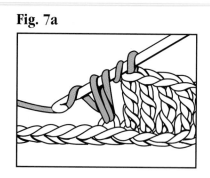

Fig. 7b

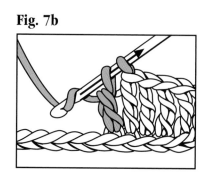

DOUBLE TREBLE CROCHET
(abbreviated dtr)

YO 3 times, insert hook in stitch or space indicated, YO and pull up a loop *(Fig. 8a)*, (YO and draw through 2 loops on hook) 4 times *(Fig. 8b)*.

Fig. 8a

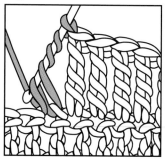

Fig. 8b

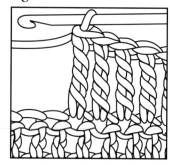

PATTERN STITCHES

CLUSTER

A Cluster can be worked all in the same stitch or space *(Figs. 9a & b)*, **or** across several stitches *(Figs. 9c & d)*.

Fig. 9a

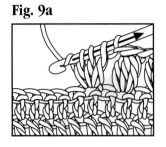

Fig. 9b

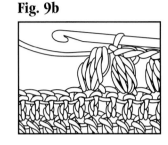

Fig. 9c

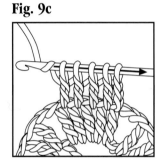

Fig. 9d

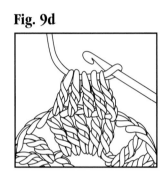

POPCORN

Work specified number of dc in stitch or space indicated, drop loop from hook, insert hook in first dc of dc group, hook dropped loop and draw through *(Figs. 10a & b)*.

Fig. 10a   4-dc Popcorn

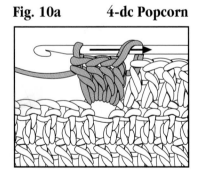

Fig. 10b   5-dc Popcorn

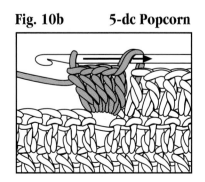

PUFF STITCH

★ YO, insert hook in stitch indicated, YO and pull up a loop even with loop on hook; repeat from ★ 2 times **more**, YO and draw through all 7 loops on hook *(Fig. 11)*, ch 1 to close.

Fig. 11

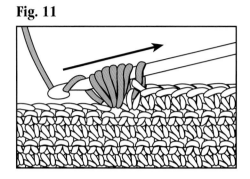

POST STITCH

Work around post of stitch indicated, inserting hook in direction of arrow *(Fig. 12)*.

Fig. 12

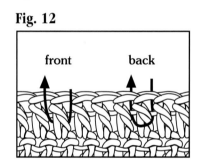

FRONT POST DOUBLE CROCHET
(abbreviated FPdc)

YO, insert hook from **front** to **back** around post of stitch indicated *(Fig. 12)*, YO and pull up a loop (3 loops on hook) *(Fig. 13)*, (YO and draw through 2 loops on hook) twice.

Fig. 13

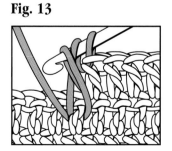

BACK POST DOUBLE CROCHET
(abbreviated BPdc)

YO, insert hook from **back** to **front** around post of stitch indicated *(Fig. 12, page 137)*, YO and pull up a loop (3 loops on hook) *(Fig. 14)*, (YO and draw through 2 loops on hook) twice.

Fig. 14

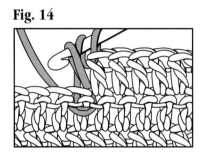

FRONT POST TREBLE CROCHET
(abbreviated FPtr)

YO twice, insert hook from **front** to **back** around post of stitch indicated *(Fig. 12, page 137)*, YO and pull up a loop (4 loops on hook) *(Fig. 15)*, (YO and draw through 2 loops on hook) 3 times.

Fig. 15

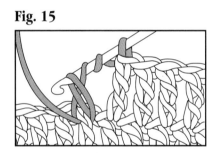

FRONT POST DOUBLE TREBLE
CROCHET *(abbreviated FPdtr)*

YO 3 times, insert hook from **front** to **back** around post of stitch indicated *(Fig. 12, page 137)*, YO and pull up a loop (5 loops on hook) *(Fig. 16)*, (YO and draw through 2 loops on hook) 4 times.

Fig. 16

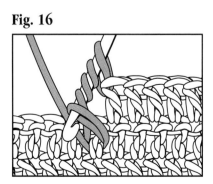

REVERSE SINGLE CROCHET
(abbreviated reverse sc)

Working from **left** to **right**, insert hook in stitch to right of hook *(Fig. 17a)*, YO and draw through, under and to left of loop on hook (2 loops on hook) *(Fig. 17b)*, YO and draw through both loops on hook *(Fig. 17c)* (**reverse sc made, Fig. 17d**).

Fig. 17a

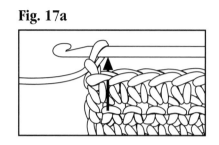

Fig. 17b

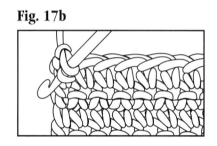

Fig. 17c

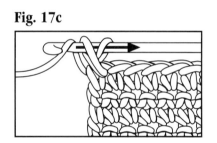

Fig. 17d

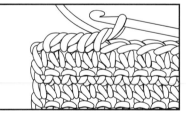

BASIC AFGHAN STITCH

Note: Each row is worked in 2 steps, working to the left picking up loops and then working to the right completing each stitch.

Row 1 - Step 1: Working in Top Loops Only, insert hook in second ch from hook *(Fig. 2c, page 135)*, YO and pull up a loop (2 loops on hook), pull up a loop in each ch across *(Fig. 18)*, keeping all loops on hook.

DO NOT TURN WORK. The side facing you is the **right** side.

Fig. 18

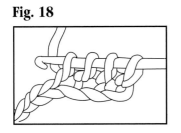

Row 1 - Step 2: YO and draw through one loop **(beginning Afghan St made)**, ★ YO and draw through 2 loops on hook **(Afghan St made, *Fig. 19*)**; repeat from ★ across until one loop remains on hook. This is the first stitch of the next row.

Note: These two steps are always counted as one row.

Fig. 19

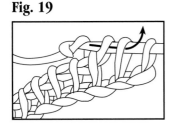

Row 2 - Step 1: Insert hook through upright bar of second loop *(Fig. 20a)*, YO and pull up a loop (2 loops on hook). Pull up a loop in each bar across to last bar. For a firmer edge, insert hook through last bar and the strand behind it *(Fig. 20b)*, YO and pull up a loop.

Fig. 20a   **Fig. 20b**

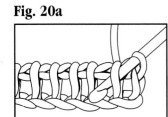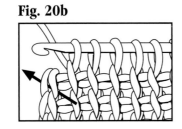

Row 2 - Step 2: Work same as Row 1 - Step 2.

Repeat Row 2 throughout.

Bind off Row: ★ Insert hook through bar, YO and draw loosely through bar **and** loop on hook **(slip st made)**; repeat from ★ across; do **not** finish off.

CROSS STITCH ON AFGHAN STITCH

The embroidery is worked by following a chart. Each square on the chart represents one complete cross stitch.
Cross Stitches are worked over the upright bar of the Afghan Stitch *(Fig. 21)*. If you find it difficult to see where to work the cross stitches, hold the Block at each side and pull slightly. Evenly spaced holes will be apparent on each side of the upright bars.

Fig. 21

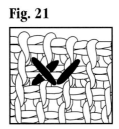

Look carefully at your work and you will see that the stitches in the Edging are worked into the slip stitch row at the top and into the chain at the bottom. This does not take away any part of the area over which you will be embroidering. However, at the sides, the Edging affects the number of bars which can be used for embroidery.

Thread a needle with an 18" strand of yarn. Hold Block with **right** side facing and marked edge at top. Count to find the bar where you wish to begin. Bring needle up from back of work through first hole, leaving a 3" end on back. Work over this end to secure. Bring needle down through hole diagonally across, pulling stitch flat against fabric, but not so tight as to pucker the fabric. You have now made one half of a cross stitch. You can either complete that stitch now or work across an area in half crosses and then work back, crossing them as you go. Just be sure that the top half of every cross stitch is worked in the same direction.
Finish off by weaving end of yarn under several stitches; cut close to work.

STITCHING TIPS

JOINING WITH SC

When instructed to join with sc, begin with a slip knot on hook. Insert hook in stitch or space indicated, YO and pull up a loop, yarn over and draw through both loops on hook.

BACK OR FRONT LOOP ONLY

Work only in loop(s) indicated by arrow *(Fig. 22)*.

Fig. 22

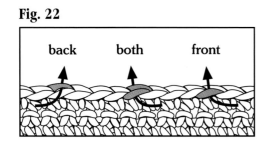

FREE LOOPS

After working in Back or Front Loops Only on a row or round, there will be a ridge of unused loops. These are called the free loops. Later, when instructed to work in the free loops of the same row or round, work in these loops *(Fig. 23a)*.
When instructed to work in a free loop of a beginning chain, work in loop indicated by arrow *(Fig. 23b)*.

Fig. 23a   **Fig. 23b**

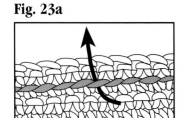   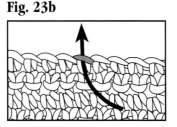

CHANGING COLORS

Work the last stitch to within one step of completion, hook new yarn *(Fig. 24a)* and draw through loops on hook. Cut old yarn and work over both ends unless otherwise specified.
When working in rounds, drop old yarn and join with slip stitch to first stitch using new yarn *(Fig. 24b)*.

Fig. 24a

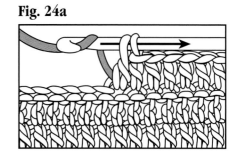

Fig. 24b

NO-SEW JOINING

Hold Squares or Motifs with **wrong** sides together. Slip st or sc into space as indicated *(Fig. 25)*.

Fig. 25

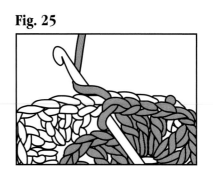

WORKING IN SPACE BEFORE STITCH

When instructed to work in space **before** a stitch or in spaces **between** stitches, insert hook in space indicated by arrow *(Fig. 26)*.

Fig. 26

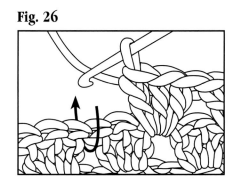

WEAVING IN YARN ENDS

Good finishing techniques make a big difference in the quality of any crocheted piece. Make a habit of taking care of loose ends as you work. **Never** tie a knot in your yarn. They may poke through to the right side and will sometimes come untied and unravel. Weaving in the ends gives a much better result. Thread a yarn needle with the yarn end. With **wrong** side facing, weave the needle through several stitches, then reverse the direction and weave it back through several more stitches. When the end is secure, clip the yarn off close to your work.

You may also hide your ends as you work by crocheting over them for several inches to secure, then weave in opposite direction; clip the remaining lengths off close to your work. Always check your work to be sure the yarn ends do not show on the right side.

HOW TO DETERMINE THE RIGHT SIDE

Many designs are m___ ___ ___ ___ ___ he **right** side. Notice ___ ___ ___ ___ ___ *. 27a)* and the **back** ___ ___ ___ ___ ___ ___ ___ ___ __sy identification, ___ ___ ___ ___ ___ ___ ___ __ce of yarn around any stitc___ ___ ___ ___.

Fig. 27a

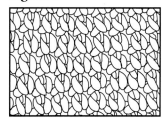

Fig. 27b

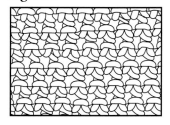

EDGING
SINGLE CROCHET EVENLY ACROSS OR AROUND

When instructed to single crochet evenly across or around, the single crochets should be spaced to keep the piece lying flat. Work a few single crochets at a time, checking periodically to be sure your edge is not distorted. If the edge is puckering, you need to add a few more single crochets; if the edge is ruffling, you need to remove some single crochets. Keep trying until the edge lies smooth and flat.

FINISHING

WHIPSTITCH

With **wrong** sides together, and beginning in corner stitch, sew through both pieces once to secure the beginning of the seam, leaving an ample yarn end to weave in later. Insert needle from **front** to **back** through **both** loops of **each** piece *(Fig. 28a)* **or** through **inside** loops *(Fig. 28b)*. Bring needle around and insert it from **front** to **back** through the next loops of **both** pieces. Continue in this manner across to corner, keeping the sewing yarn fairly loose.

Fig. 28a

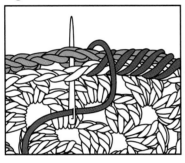

Fig. 28b

FRINGE

Cut a piece of cardboard 8" wide and ¹/₂" longer than desired fringe. Wind the yarn **loosely** and **evenly** around the length of the cardboard until the card is filled, then cut across one end; repeat as needed. Align the number of strands desired and fold in half.

With **wrong** side facing and using a crochet hook, draw the folded end up through a stitch, row, or loop, and pull the loose ends through the folded end *(Figs. 29a & b)*; draw the knot up **tightly** *(Fig. 29c & d)*. Repeat, spacing as specified. Lay flat on a hard surface and trim the ends.

Fig. 29a

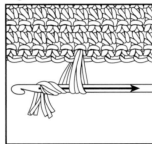

Fig. 29b

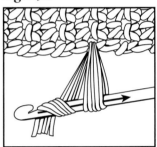

Fig. 29c

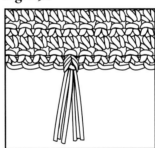

Fig. 29d

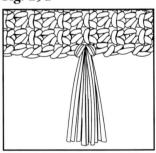

credits

To Magna IV Color Imaging of Little Rock, Arkansas, we say thank you for the superb color reproduction and excellent pre-press preparation.

We want to especially thank photographers Ken West, Larry Pennington, Mark Mathews, and Karen Shirey of Peerless Photography, Little Rock, Arkansas, and Jerry R. Davis of Jerry Davis Photography, Little Rock, Arkansas, for their time, patience, and excellent work.

We would like to extend a special word of thanks to the talented designers who created the lovely projects in this book:

Eleanor Albano: *Easter Eggs*, page 44
Alexander-Stratton: *Lilac Lane*, page 58
Mary Lamb Becker: *Orchid Whimsy,* page 46, and *Harvest Home*, page 120
Carla Bentley: *Primarily for Kids*, page 100
Judy Bolin: *Sweet Hearts*, page 22; *Country Plaid*, page 26; and *Grandmother's Garden*, page 48
Carol Brill: *Hugs & Kisses*, page 20
Rose Marie Brooks: *Rose Garden*, page 98
Louella Cartwright: *Country Lane*, page 90
John H. Feddersen, Jr.: *Father's Favorite*, page 64
Marion Graham: *Patchwork Stars*, page 12
Anne Halliday: *Baby's Rainbow Granny*, page 28; *Tulip Kisses*, page 30; *Darling Daisies*, page 56; *America*, page 82; *Waves of Grain*, page 86; and *Golden Rule*, page 94
Irene Johnson: *St. Patrick's Wrap*, page 34
Terry Kimbrough: *Aran Comfort*, page 8; *Roses Remembered*, page 68; *Wedding Ring*, page 70; and *Victorian Summer*, page 88
Ann Kirtley: *Baby's Keepsake*, page 52, and *Milady's Fans*, page 54
Melissa Leapman: *Warm Tradition*, page 108; *Evergreen Inspiration*, page 122; and *Majestic Pine*, page 128
Ingrid Nielsen: *Campfire Blanket*, page 110
Irma Park: *Cozy Appeal*, page 126
Carole Prior: *Frosty Flowers*, page 6; *Wintry Day*, page 10; *Love Songs*, page 18; *Field of Daffodils*, page 32; *Carefree Cover-up*, page 76; *Ocean Breeze*, page 80; *Autumn Blaze*, page 106; *Rich Fall Stripes*, page 114; *Hayride Wrap*, page 116; and *Team Spirit*, page 118
Mary Jane Protus: *Summer Shells*, page 78
Rena V. Stevens: *Bride's Lace*, page 66
Carole Rutter Tippett: *Rodeo Stars*, page 96, and *Blanket of Snow*, page 124
Maggie Weldon: *Brown-Eyed Susans*, page 84, and *Magnificent Mums*, page 112